Songs and Stories
of the Ghouls

Wesleyan Poetry

Songs and Stories of the Ghouls

ALICE NOTLEY

WESLEYAN UNIVERSITY PRESS

MIDDLETOWN, CONNECTICUT

Wesleyan University Press

Middletown CT 06459

www.wesleyan.edu/wespress

© 2011 by Alice Notley

Manufactured in the United States of America

Wesleyan University Press is a member of the Green Press Initiative.
The paper used in this book meets their minimum requirement for
recycled paper.

5 4 3 2 1

Library of Congress Cataloging-in-Publication Data

Notley, Alice, 1945–

Songs and stories of the ghouls / Alice Notley.

p. cm. — (Wesleyan poetry)

ISBN 978-0-8195-6956-1 (cloth : alk. paper) — ISBN 978-0-8195-7153-3 (e-book)

1. Title.

PS3564.O79S66   2011

811'.54—dc23   2011023518

Excerpts from this book were first published in *Crowd*, *The Canary*,
Superflux, *5 Trope*, *Interim*, *The Café Review*, *VLAK*, *Denver
Quarterly*, *Skein*, *caliphabet*, and *The New Review of Literature*.
A selection of poems from the opening section, "Introducing Carthage,"
was first published in *Grave of Light, New and Selected Poems 1970–2005*
(Wesleyan University Press, 2006). The poem "Another Part of Now"
first appeared as Backwoods Broadsides, Chaplet Series #94.

NATIONAL
ENDOWMENT
FOR THE ARTS
A great nation
deserves great art.

This project is supported in part by an award from
the National Endowment for the Arts

Contents

INTRODUCING
CARTHAGE

There was power in that room. I saw
it, because my eyes were crushed out

It's my judgment   on this almost face
holding the mouth   so.

The scars on my right side won't fail.
I've come back wearing them
instead of a conscience or a guide

in order to cause
                    a breakaway culture.

trembling white   vertical lines
in black sky   above sea. they
spell what it   might be; the

emotional   tone of the old
universe   was vicious.
it had no   care for me

≈

Who matters it died. There will be no abrogation of this face you can find
it in the ground. The magic and on its part I utter anything know it's in my
unlawful hand for I choose a form not easily seen. Face is my own it may
look demons but is not a side like this place where they want to walk over
and over until all in the ground is fast dead. The light between letters will
become in my unlawful hand the conversant weapon so you'll let me destroy
your intentions.

The face is not kindly. I am dark and in profile to election pervading the fabric and in need of demolition. You still can't see me, thinking there's a collective utility. But there is a chaos if I so choose.

Half of a scarlet rose burst back of the screen behind which your layers are shed. The feeble radiation of quotidian appeasement: it would be necessary to get through the time segment so the scarlet becomes more intense and the murders may go on. I use this against them.

~

Was supposed to be endlessly
interested. I don't want you.
driving towards the danger
coast, I don't want you. I won't
remember the beckoning grant.
Won't remember the grave. I
don't want you.

Screamed burned ripped
    It is a fracture that at first
is taken for a joke. because it's
your first break. heavens
        the servant of memory explodes.
        creation have done with it. No.
it's not even old. or odd. and when
no word works
        there can be no notification.
        I have the wrong in my hand.
this handle staggers and loses
        its furnished shape. how much

4

interest they pay (is that what interest
is?)
        I have this hapless caught. I
might have caught it already
        remember me cries hooker.
no she's up on the hook. still in the
days of looker and ken.
        don't you think you ought
to arrive? if you're traveling.
        I was finding the middle of the
handle, howling. if it remembers me
at all. and if it does, leave, I think so.

≈

The ghoul-girl. There was one to care for, but I can't remember the name.

The ghoul. Care about the bodies again.

You will always be the ghoul-girl now.

To stagger and live; a moonstone will fill the head.

I see their thoughts. They are round and white and constitute the power. If you drop your thought, you fail. And if you let some fall, and if you let some spill, you are facing it.

It leaks out and faces you dead. But I keep loving myself she said.

She will walk me to sleep.

She walks me to sleep.

I bore a child said she and cruel to see it perceived as I. Walking here where the city's open to ghouls.

You find that magic is dreadful.

It's all that I have.

You are the ghoul-child.

It was carved on all the walls: no one sees it. No one sees me.

This is a luminous quality. I'm the ghoul; because it's what I say.

Because it's what I say, I'm in love with that.

≈

I'm standing where no one sees me; a reasonable object. I could be about
    anything but I'm not.
An encomium, they're everywhere stone white women.
I keep doing the other one; keep not being the one in question. Not the
    woman in question.
Well search home. I shall a ghost be dead.
The real woman would say real things.
I scorn to come from your scepter; she will help you express this ville where
    your shack is on schedule.
I don't want to be the real woman.

I remember a word 'we would meet again.'
I'm not the real we.
I was trained to risk you efficiently he might say.
In the arena of the civilian. No one important is one. But is a ghoul a civilian?
The wind blows through this stall for better to lock me in the outside of
    everything.
The inscribed words for the known crimes change. Can you keep up? There
    are so many. Who is the audience for your person?
It's burning into my forehead.

≈

What she reports against you isn't
what she reproaches you for
Building presses through windows,
faces of who you betray. It's all
in a store front now, everything is.
When you protest, you're no
longer a civilian: they can kill you.
I've come back without anyone to
snitch to, I must really be dead. You
can't bribe me if you can't see me.
"I've killed hundreds in honor of
you." Cooking the books so alive
was that way. Coin after coin in the old
pay phone to hell. "Listen to my music . . ."

≈

If anything hurts I'll suppress someone pushing my lace.
If they offer everyone drugs so you can go visit your
friend to forget that the sheets are soaked. That's
some nurturing blood, he said. I was shot through. They
hire people to take care of it so you'll continue to support

the red flood; cloth, I was whole cloth saturate. No one
will ever forget you stet. Can you find my face yet?
The power gathers around broken windows. It witnesses
the overthrow each time one destroys Rome from within
the sepulcher of Carthage. How do you do that I open this

mouth *Delenda est.*

≈

The city I founded I will found again. Running through the cards, you've used all the cards up. The city I founded I will found again. These are the new ghoulish cards with their own magic lice made licit. Suit of blood, suit of crania, suit of viral obbligatos, suit of blunting salt. The city I founded I will found again. And as in those days was there not found so false a lover going on the ground as whose power I will slay this new city's burning into my forehead. I can't see it, give me something, you can have dread. Can I have justice? Never, what can I have this new city burning into my forehead.

∼

Felix the fortunate and how was this city first purchased? A woman who founded it said to be betrayed as if no matter your courage you're only haunted by sex. There was always another story a different form of betrayal. She will enter the country desperate powerfully cognizant, she has done this. Remonstrance guilt is freezing me inside the ghoul tatters midnight glass but I'll be frequent and not stand aside even a monster can found a city don't ask me to open up I'm out here. This is what I can give you back we were invaded assimilated tossed but now are not repugnant to each other because called 'lost.' I already know this song but I've already founded this city before when I've forgotten all the rest streets fire opal so you see. There's no moisture in here because I never cry, you say I don't know which part I'd be supposed to cry for. A tear became a rate of exchange for goods of recognition but that was before the new founding; so what is the name of this city? Is it really Carthage; I think that name will do for now. Do you haunt it to devour our condition again speaking this older way it's been so done but I've never been *here* before.

≈

I know what happened to you; I know
you can hardly stand
I never did anything but run from
the phantoms in *your* head.
You cost me my house and body
when I come back a Medea
to haunt your controls I'm no
poor girl now; have you ever seen a
black cape like this? I can still
shake you up by pressing my finger
to your chest, now that you're
old enough to have failed at the good.
Oh haven't you? What do you know
except for this haunt I am?

≈

The whole story was a *late* lie. Why would she kill KEPT her children? In this *we cite* city she didn't; WE know what's true and not the tradition a blood of misbegotten treason. Scars tell a different story in high voice *I was possessed* by the creations of a lurid culture spear obsessive they came to take. No this is over and the scars say *don't remember*, though don't you? *Can you make our art* they say? Shadows the scars pronounce *think with us*.

~

I had no love at that time and wore

Is the color bad for me (black) and
he said you should dress like the others and I said I'm not like the others. I
wasn't looking for clarity. I've never known anyone whose mind was clearer
than mine.

He left her because he could always get another one. Or he is trying to
kill me to have everything I should have the smallest part of if at all. They
weep for the cut-up women in their documents as if they wanted to kill to
grieve. The difference is that I'm slipping back further to try to search for
my own. I'm sure I can find my documents.

How have you escaped destruction I am always on a trajectory going back
I'm in time differently from you. In one sense I survive by having been
eradicated and if your culture has been razed you will understand me. The
magic is always in my hands and in my crushed-out eyes whatever is deleted
returns.

~

On the banks of whose kindness, nowhere, they blindly struck with hands
that the fires leap, when I of the earth and the overturning of prayers took
my blankets and entered in order to face the other ghosts or ghouls. I knew
our arts could make life bearable: I must be nothing I have been in recent

times. I will mix a potion for our use a substance to prevent the present as it has been known— your present— for hasn't there always been another one transpiring? The murders are already done but since we are already ghosts from them aren't they eradicated now? I must remember a new past and not the old present. This document records a possibility of power back here, which I have access to by betraying my old life and entering that camp where I won't remember my details. Already I speak of the fact that life was never new, but as I have returned to another past, may it renew. It has a thousand wide approaches and gates open on all sides many more than four where I imagine I have always plied my craft.

~

I am warriors   warriors warriors

Critic of parts the plaintiff
It remains to be seen if the designs in your hair
are permanent, inflicting an identity or
beauty—which is it—of plaits and paths
        above your eyes.

Do you have to be a warrior? I ask her
I'll find you again before I'm finished
and we'll fight them, because we can't
imagine another cure for our resentment
she says, it's what pushes me on

I hear someone screaming out here
but she's recorded speech to be sampled
by who makes her his: he's gone

I never want to see you again but I want to
sing this song

~

There's still an assault on my shadow. A tree with symbols hanging from it.
In my own self or structure. You can't be omitted for I'm a protective object.
The inscription all over me places you near a home. They kill you off and
tell of their map bleeding from your forehead. But anything can protect us.
I took the child and enfolded her in my flatness so she wouldn't be harmed.
See to this crime they said; the object I am drew the child even further into
itself, for justice would never help her. As everything seems to be a made
thing, when I make this for you, out of the same mouth anything comes
from. I'm holding you as close as I can. I cover you.

~

What were you doing when I thought you were dead, weren't you dead? The
history of Carthage has been related by numerous ancient men but the
Tyrian princess Dido founder of the city cannot be mentioned except in
relation to her tragic passion for Aeneas; an important production of little
masks characterizes the Punic world you are hellenized you worship Deme-
ter and Kore. The young woman is dressed in a skirt of folded wings upon
her sarcophagus our knowledge of the religion is lacunar but it is possible

that one worshipped nothing except for untrue but powerful images and symbols perhaps 'worship' means 'use' as it should. Was there once again but this time I knew he was really dead there is a poem in the scars on my liver a written history or map which is beautiful but only covers me I must be the child who isn't listening so I'll hear. Destroyed in 146 B.C. your poetry is dreadful, vacant and inept and ours will survive as long as our empire lasts: every present writer says. Towards changes hands of configuration each small mask is a word to cover your lack that is where language stands on no foundation but the wars it has always upheld for if your ways were destroyed and your poems broken and ploughed into the salted earth what would you be? The ghoulishness of this project is affirmed by any style and there is no 'way forward' but your empire's way.

~

If you meet me here I was Lady
if I meet you where you were killed
then I'm no longer a civilian if I was
your drug. There's nothing to replace what

you need from the soil; salted it's perfect
your Lady. If you meet me here. (say the scars)
If I met you as Lady, the senses of
where you are now; if I met you without

a conscience: why should I have one
when you're asking me to assuage yours?
The gas is always free when you're dead.
There's no money where you meet me, too bad.

~

Millions of bodies winged ghouls or souls is there enough space for them here as they return? Insects engraving themselves into pages they keep coming back. Someone says, *she has to be dreaming so you'll see me.* Do you see the small masks? Small since so many have died; and so many of their words have disappeared. The conqueror language is struggling with the masks but doesn't want to break them, doesn't want old breath to escape. In the form of a sign, because I wear the white skin of a ghoul. You don't know what I mean, do you? You don't know what any of us mean.

~

Turned away, the art is to
incorporate myself
    into this shape
Can you see an army's needs
can you see a leg blown off
What do an army's needs look like
name the future tense sign
in the first conjugation

a beautiful adjacent inflection
    flexing the
knee of a woman, myself
sure to make up such separate
    words as
leg and self
why should I leave myself out
when I'm not here

she gave the last kisses to them
but they will have omitted her
first chaos containing, you say,
the sounds of land mines exploding
and greater explosions, more
      pieces tossed
what do an army's needs look like
flesh chunks whirled round in hurricane

                ~

Walking away turns to look over shoulder in black dragging power out of
time pursed lips less disapproving in the tornout robe along the strand.
Someone decided, for you, to destroy Carthage or Corinth, make you weak
a beautiful invention of the owners for you. Where the beauty is, take some
and use it against them. If they invented it take some. Is she willful though
right away a compiler of fates I will use, who can't get a job at the bureau.
She's pulling power away from his torso, leaving. I'm inclined to use you
myself, motivated mask. It was my city first, and I found it before you could
rule, because your secrets were mechanical. You'll have to beg for it from me,
you'll have to come backwards behind your own words because there's no
picture of you. A curse was invoked with great solemnity upon anyone who
might attempt to rebuild the city. Is that a picture? You were so barren you
couldn't hear the beauty in the scratches when twigs dragged against the
panes on the other side of old records. I lived with whatever you said
because I could sing it, the sources say. The ruins ploughed to express final
destruction I WILL tell in the recitative of misery and fury what you do to

me still. Even backwards can she know different word if the salt's ploughed in. But all words are different without their masks.

≈

You don't know who you've been
at any meddling or desperate
        point
the nerves I'm displaying along
my back, to be here, are they it
that is how I think wordlessly
but I still have to tell you, as if
you're me, centuries of distinctions
the woman in the hardcase views
        the worms archly
you named it, I didn't, fascist smiling
        runt
I remember enough of this
        to ensure my phrasing
But I've never been anyone I knew
You're not used to you's you really are

≈

Black sequins compression. Only the pressure is certain, lay this next to another. She'll turn around on initial discomfort. The sequins are appealing, beside the violets that are paper seals. At first it was too compressed, so I've diffused it she says. I'm looking back at the future so it won't hurt with its depravity, dead man. And no one went with me that smooth because these jewels when nothing cost. Don't you see that once there was no cost, because there wasn't really a compression, because there were shiny sequins. There's something I have to destroy. Place the humble sequins next to the light waves I'm in struggle takes the eyes. She takes a mask to use its eyes I remember this— have eyes for light posed a given. You needed to see, if you were a maid. She took the light and broke it as hard as she could so you couldn't tell it. The black disks scattered deaths of details to place there all the change I had.

~

Flat gold the color's no longer in her clothing
it's in you. This is what they used to call light,
when light was a story. Now you don't know
if it exists: does it? I'm stripping the conqueror's
word: From the secret of my body to the desert
of my feet what color I can't follow as if it were
light or you. That's because I broke everything.
You're what they used to call light, when light
was what *they* kept making. It isn't there anymore.
See inside the lower spine of the pianist his back's
cut open. I watch what they once called nerves
move as he plays learning to think. We're
redefining relation not looking at each other.

~

I stand here in whose eyes
the name of light is audience
burning into my forehead
waitresses' voices along the spine
if what was once light
        isn't
        my audience
what are you doing to me?
who was I broken for
was it worth it to be?

If I'm a shade
        acting
what once will occur
it must be for the song I wore
hear what they all said to you
a gesture or tone: someone lies
in the intentional tongue
betraying you again and again
        the one
        or the many
whose thoughts I stand here before

Because there's no light, what an
        outrage
was made of the science
of definitions
like what happened to me
performing here in a mad scene
        not
        and never mad
I hadn't seen clearly until I enacted her

≈

So stay before the beginning it is a ghoul. It's hard, she said. I'm walking as ghoul towards the shore again to show you my magic face for the beauty song may be produced from horror if you've been there and come backwards what else do you know? Outside my body's perceived worth I'm interested in the shape made by my omission from the lists, such omissions or holes are filled though no one sees them. What song am I singing while I'm not here in my dead rags in my solitude? The power's in those empty spaces such as solitude and missing body parts. Dorsally he knows the words dear lord above bring back why articulate those so he thinks past no-love's meanness in the language of the submerged words but sing now your song in due order. All things are the gift of the earth, which, too, is not here, but I the omitted one am this flight which provides you with a presence more real than life though only her voice and bones remain to this gaunt one.

∽

Where city arises from salt flats
I must have walked out of a station
to see it, pale blue, with birds
whose cathedral not mine from
before the salt and before;
but I have something to do here for you.
Came back to life but hadn't
minded being extinguished and would be
again, as cities disappear along the
dead shore; I was too frightened, then,
to hear her clearly. But I believe this
city is where I see and hear best.
Having bypassed the origin of man

~

It's an echo of everything you've ever done. I know and that's its meaning.
Before we were covered with echoing eyes was the first echo pure? Who was
first conquered, they say you spoke no worthy language. Salt from every pore
and each a primary mask or echo of you. But when the light is broken up
you can't hide behind it. She gave it back to the places no one can conquer.
If this word hurts my mouth it's because it has no mask on, and something
of it is indigenous but not assigned for nothing's assigned. We know no one
holds ground; we are the founding ghouls of this nation.

~

Woman with antlers, deer-headed antlered woman in black against black
lace, black-headed deer woman, Lady of the mountains whose antlers melt
into lace. Lady of the mountains, emerges from my right side and all the
lacy scars there, why is she a deer? Because I'm not anthropomorphic, soul
of the mountain night. This is my echo from before, from what I had made
for you vocally, and from before we acceded to the time line never like lace.
Lady the mountain middle of no spatial universe. I have the antlers she says
which extend from the deer head in the middle of our echo. Lady of Wild
Animals, for whom the animals return, the deer with the heart or breath
line, through the mouth to the center echoing. Do you hear the words of the
conquerors or do you hear the voices of deer? echoes, can you find a center

in an echo. I'm finding, with the finder, the antlers paths leading from my

head. I am the center of it, the center of the lady.

~

Do you think you had to be able to
speak or sing, in order to go mad?
in which language did a woman
once first approach that barrier
before we drowned in your alphabet

They will cast my child into the sea.
Have they ever done differently
through cypresses return to my home
having the same ultimate
sign, so that I can be a woman

example of their tables and diagrams
I call on the soul of decipherment
to strip power from their dream
and give it to mine. In black on the strand
where detritus hardens into beauty

anything I hold—a pearl in each hand—
protects me from their words. They say that I . . .
but I didn't. They say that I—but in
the old language I is who speaks to her-
self, in images and carvings of sounds.

Will always serve a meal with the
fingerbones of a child mixed in—He can't
help it? but I can help what I—
I screamed at the forecast to change
the letters of the deaths. Change them back

to natural forms in my eyes first given.
I am holding her from before
your distribution of mines
I don't know how to concur
and never will, without blood frigid

in my wounds. Song to aid secrets
quaeque magos, Tellus, I have willed
te quoque, traho. I. Mad as grief,
slaughter your decipherment. If I
kill so you can't have, am I even seen?

That you wrote me lectures as soon as
you counted. I want this song
to betray history, since history's now mine.
Personnel surround the mine
which itself appears to be singing

as if it were Medea or Dido, the same
mouth from which comes anything
power I have, to you the
material voice, whose control
means your destruction.

~

Like a scratchy record—my documents are recorded on old equipment.

If there is nothing to do but enfold you in transparent plastic and watch

you breathe, you, baby, so I can get better, it's because it's all I was born for.

If none of the new words are true to you, the old ones each spread out,

into scratchy encirclings, she said to attack the center of the note, but the

note could be anywhere I implore.

The pattern ripped where we won't weave it so she walks here stalking the role which she still wants to sing in no light but that inside the record. Isn't that story all gone, itself

and you believed

she was a murderer, not a magician: as soldiers slip inside us and tell no spell but unilingual chant along the blade

I am the scratchy spell

document not inside words but centers of notes to disappear through black sequins. She's still alive

does she know it?

They want us to know what they said; they all want us to recognize them.

I only recognize baby breathing

each note. They want me to leave her the new Medea. They're afraid because they don't know these words though words familiar as ghouls along the shore sing I am beauty to the ghoul chant sister.

Accept this magic note.

≈

If there's change you put it into this sculpture's slot the room where once before Carthage we're not in the named light, soldier. In this gold the other side of a word like bear or not to be borne unless you make up nerves for it but in the shadow-nerves this song. For that breakthrough into the Shadow, we the dead and mutilated the defective dip our hands. Let Mavis in,

without obligation face most all the beautiful face. I am the most beautiful
face said a ghoul one down, you have promoted the whore until it's still.
Every whore in the history collection come forward with his face of a
woman to find if he were beautiful so Mavis sing. He had shaved skull to
make a shape under the wind but there's no real wind. I would have been
placed wherever you wanted to kill some, for I have long use and no signa-
ture; am I glad you'll be dead too, nameless no-record or no-document; put
to head hard-liner calls for a shoot, always calling. But there is no bloodfill
of ticks here of wisdom so say what they took from you in order to keep
their own mien with mine they'd say to any linguistic heiress or bird. This is
the shade of that thrush leave it alone. I can't calculate the arrows in time
you thought you were whole but didn't know now there's only narrow to a
single expansion your little death as viewed by the times bolstered by them
successful with one's death the real shadow Mavis sings, that's what the
power called it till I took power we the shadow I saw heads and fingers,
hands, push up through the soil. That was us, so Mavis sings.

~

the commanders regret life's brevity for themselves their parent beard
they are the class thousand wars to whom only comes the elusive spring
came not to me magician though I broke the gods of their procuration
startled the common places ripped to bear up their navy or oral possession
they neither rule me nor sequester my bitterest regnum of itinerant fact
I arrived to make fold of auric tendancy in the atmospheric transverse
unturned to necessitate honesty's pay while they cynically bade us
address a plaint to feigned arbitration assemble and expend in invention

primarily to please the fleet not the deep, oh fasten up smoothly
your accessible beauty its unnecessary and illimitable mode
you are the conquerors paying no one, being vantage's own surly breath
being the simplest invective mantled in the letters of victorious lead

~

Reprise. No prize.
I'm in a store that's everywhere
food on the shelves, bread; but
who does this part of experience
          serve?

That you allow me to eat
That you think you allow me to think:
have implanted thoughts in my head:
that if you don't extinguish me you will
substitute for my savings—
          my own love—
your images. Technologists with youth blonde

cruel. I have to learn you, waiting to *see*
within me whatever you've placed:
lies made material visions not mine.
As you have declared my emotion: that which
your poems incarnate—my supposed emptiness
of intellect to be possessed by your commodious

greed: is there enough territory within me, for you?
          never
enough room for a torturer.

~

I was in flames. They were only lines, it was only a drawing. I left the drawing back there, for years, several drawings of a girl myself always burning. Because of the old stove? a quotation. The flames are straight lines fire drawn by me. I crawled through the magic flames, pulled myself through and left the east side of the more remote continent. If you've chosen wrongly; or did someone implant an image in you? How innocent your very purposes I find indeed: said the soldier to the fire. In this document we record how purple was first mixed by shooting red and blue sacs with a gun. Or rubbed matte paint on her nipples, so no one would see them; and if you bleed you've been reared on blood; you musn't soothsay with numbers the laic convergence of six lines in my own breath, natural lines, that is, rather straight not precise in the later way. The oncoming tempest has been invoked in its beauty because it's us, and I must have always contributed to the cause. Whose words are these? Child, they can touch the glass to your forehead, to make an incision for their implant; or I'll stand on the convergence of the lines until I speak truly. I was in flames but they were lines, burning me up with change or chance though I did nothing but not do. The parallel fiery lines that have been altered to converge within one alone. It is roughly where all location trembles emotively. If the continent they found of self-hatred has no biologic basis, I can turn the flames outward, having been the target as one until continent collapse. It exists in my regard and if you kill me it is dead the woman said. I know where I am now. All art has for its origin

∿

Justice may appear in the
guise of a hard, devious mother
I want shoes for my baby
son my werewolf son

None of you can sing a song
The best you can do is breathe
every breath opining
following the prescribed instrument

which is now a hatchet
Justice has Egyptian hair because
you'll be dead; she wants ten
dollars from you; I've offered mine

None of you sing; you beg for each
other's love in chopped-up phrases:
every breath opining a duty to
the gods of the times, whose times

Justice isn't a pleasant woman
Her baby has a wolfish face that only
I could love; the Egyptian gods
have animal heads don't they: the

dead man loves Justice's baby
Having had his soul weighed by her
Take your backpack off, it's in the
way, she says gruffly; he plays

with her hairy baby. I'm trying
to tell you, the Law knows you're
as wise as a wolf; only the baby
is important; only I can sing

the Law that hard and devious woman
says that this is just. You have
given birth to another wild hybrid
like yourself. I'm following you to your

heights: I'm the only intellectual
Justice says—she's worked in peep shows—
You'll never figure me out; but
you owe my baby, and you owe me.

~

This lady was justice at the beginning: do you know the little song, that the
lady of the final order may or may not suffer your spirits dense with blood
and the rush of killing with your hands, which is natural, you say. I may not
let you in here, she says, not into my endless day, after they hang you for
their own crimes as well, condemned in their sadistic courts. Distinctions
are not of interest: further I don't know where you will go. But I'm justice,
not any of you, an abstraction live with bloody hair from my hybrid issue
at the cleft of the return I sing. Oh Mom I love you when there's blood on
your hair and you come at me railing. I entered everywhere as dispassion,
now become redheaded from judging the foul acts of your hands. I've got
bloody hair so you can love me.

~

No world is intact
and no one cares about you.

I leaned down over
don't care about, I care about
        you
I leaned down over the

world in portrayal
of carefulness, answering

something you couldn't say.
Walking or fallen and you
        were supposed
to give therapy to me—

me leaning down
brushing with painted feathers
to the left of chance your operatic,
        broken

book.

~

Can you decipher where we are if it's to be communal; or in the privacy of
this symbol, be sorry. Then where is your power? The symbol to me is pink
and spreads over the walls, comprised of large irregularly round spots for
the force of whatever I've concluded was real. I can't transform what I don't
believe in; wherever it is I've been everyone was happy except me, because

they understood the language of the forms or thought they did. Essentially I decipher an unscrupulous funerary urn full of your parts but not all of them, only the ones that you're used to—you think I'm arranging those to you the symbols of where you were. I am dressed in a certain glass predicament: that no one covers me, because I'm the marabout with a thousand teeth and vast hair; and you found magic humorous, but you died of it for you were confounded by one of your own parts, an illogic of syntax? There is a whole woman somewhere, but I have no interest in that. She would symbolize a community whereas I have tricked you so far into a dream standing where there is no light at all, and I have accepted some very expensive blood.

THE BOOK
OF DEAD

Medea ran with her children
She fled with them leaving the house where one must
accept the elaborate head in a box with its
silver and turquoise ornamentation as one's own
civilization. This severed thought will do you good
No we are leaving you. Though it was reported
she killed her children and left alone since that story
took care of all of them. Medea entrusted herself with
the remnants of her culture, in an old box. What was her
culture? You say that it was a dream, leading you on
I am the most destructive person alive because I
can't bear the lies in your heart. Every murder attributed to her
had no victim but feelings, was an assault on the sanctity of your
language covering one with the white shit of pigeons in an airshaft.

⸺

I'll take you quickly to the ghouls, we're everywhere. Or are we art; or
shattered cultures. Or, individual victims. Our paint's coming off us, dark
wormholed relics, lost poems, broken torsos beloved of museums even
before they are bombed. Old corpses.

Aren't you going to tell me about Medea? Yes. And some others. Your
version? Maybe that's it. But I have to tell you about ghouls too, I just do.
She's a ghoul. Anyone who's still around, before and after conquest, the
ongoing activity, is a ghoul. Is anyone not a ghoul?

Medea . . . but you'll want to know conventional things. You will want to
be assured, for example, that she killed Creusa, the daughter of Creon, by
sending her a poisoned dress on her wedding day. Though I've already said
that she didn't.

You don't know what you want to know, you say, but Creusa's part of the
story. Then I say, Do you really believe in poison dresses?

Because I want to be accorded . . . what's left of me. The remnants of my
culture, perhaps my personal culture. Medea *is* here. She knows it isn't that
blue head in its silver headdress hair.

One of us—myself—says: It's my statue—that means stature, that the conquerors possess now. And my best poetry's destroyed (if it's the future—who knows what time it is?) What do I care? Form has to be earned. *I* earned the form of my poems.

Who are the conquerors, you ask? Don't you know?

I still have these cultural remnants, hidden, Medea's box. Now I am Medea, about whom there are only rumors, alone again. (Children grown; on their own.) No I'm the poet too.

There is a place inside me where I hold another language close. I'm the only one who knows it. But no one wants to be such a foreigner. In all their combinations the words in my language form a statue—statute—*I know the language of one.*

The weight of passion is it. What is it for, to pass through? Keep passing through? *I am the only language I can understand.*

In the heart of almost any conqueror word, I pay for what I'm not. The parts of my body are mirrors, which fasten my soul to the earth's. But I have another soul, and still I'm a ghoul. In most respects I'm a foreigner.

Here is an example of a conqueror love song :

You stood on the ground I wanted to own
I overcame you binding you to me
I found you, love, where I wanted to be
I wanted to own you and the earth of you
I rip up the names of your ancestors and call you me
(Fill in name of country.)

To decipher Medea I go with her, as you have come here to do.

They say she founded Media: western Iran and South Azerbaijan. There are no Median records. The Medes spoke an Iranian language akin to old Persian, and one reads the Assyrian and Greek sources. Ruled Persia, captured Ninevah, united with Persia, became part of the Parthian kingdom. Later ruled by the Romans. Oh aren't you comforted by these hard facts?

How do you found a country. How do you engender a people? I think I am founding something ghoulish now.

Every bit of matter—is it matter?—is unique. What one doesn't always know is where its borders lie. But if I know the approximate borders of a spirit, speaking to it, there may be transformation: we may both be changed.

This is magic whereby I become something else and die for the moment not being a conqueror. I am a founder not a conqueror.

What do our souls expect from us in these times? That we found something, despite everything. As Dido, too, founded a city. Conquered by Rome. Conquered by posterity. But one says to any Rome, the ghouls are never conquered.

And ghouls are amassing everywhere.

In that old story Medea took out all of someone's father's blood (I can't bear to say the name) and gave his father other blood, did it for him. I used mashed plants to make new blood, rejuvenate your father. Why do that, rejuvenate the father, that power, the dynasty, why on earth? Why would you believe that?

Nothing is unchangeable except for a myth—let's change that.

Medea would never rejuvenate that father. They're all perfectly capable of rejuvenating themselves, over and over. It's what they do.

Her hair flying, some man said. And, Everything she did she did for *him* and why believe that everything, medieval writers don't. They sing that she was abandoned having left her home and culture for him for him, they—the medievals—don't believe she killed her children. Or the others.

No one really believes in her power, I assure you. She is only allowed it as an adjunct to her passion. She can't just *have* it. No woman is as yet allowed that.

*   *   *

It is a different door, it only has the frame of it, walk through. You are walking through to a *very* different culture.

It feels like I've been here before. No, been here awhile.

Somehow the light here is dreadful. I still don't know if it's light. This is surely another culture.

This is a culture where they don't have much light. At least not in Dead. They are in Dead but sometimes refer to Day; in Day would be found so-called light and the usual colors, but the spectrum isn't brilliant in Dead. Except for red; they do use that concept in Dead. Is this going too fast for you? You may want me to keep talking about Medea; I have to keep being myself; I don't know where I'm going, but I do know where I've gone. I'm here in Dead. Where else would ghouls be? And there has to be red, for blood.

I am a ghoul because I've gone on for too long, been revived too many times.

I don't want to be here, in this history, as I can't stop believing it now. It's becoming one of my documents and would be whatever I said, everything I've said that's disappeared or been ripped up is one. When I face Judgment, she has the whole transcript, the weight of my heart. I've never done a thing but I've said so much that I'm words, heart is words and there's nothing else to judge me by. Judgment is a word—she knows this, I can't stop this failure from happening, it just gets truer and truer whatever I say. That's the culture I've entered, always entered. Whatever you say is true in that moment, no lies except for everything, and a consent to go on. Leave me and go on lying, Judgment said.

This world is as convincing as the last lies everyone believed. It's as convincing as Day.

In Dead I'm allowed to believe what I please. In contradistinction to Day's lies there are the silver-red fabrications of Dead. Scary I the ghoul. I need to eat a blood-sac tonight in order to continue, as Judgment said I could. Haven't I told you about her? Or that this is a book of crime? Everything I write down will become entangled in these lies. What else would you believe? You walked through the door too.

This is the part about the blood-sac. I don't know if I want to live, but I don't know I feel like that. Until I swallow the blood-sac and suddenly want to be alive. In Dead I am told to swallow a blood-sac in order to live; it looks like the liver of a duck. I swallow it, I go on, am even reborn. Ghouls don't really die. That's one of the rules of Dead.

Medea (aren't you relieved that I've mentioned her again?), Medea is in Dead with me. Here she doesn't have to live in the standard versions of her own existence. The standard myth: did Medea kill all those people? *We* say yes. Am I dead? You're a ghoul. You used to be alive, now you're almost mythic. Who killed me? For I was dead until I swallowed the blood-sac. No one killed you. Pardon me but I know otherwise; you're deluded by the fact that I may appear as a head alone or a torso alone, you think I'm shattered art. No I've gone too fast again, I know. I look like pieced-together fragments of art, art history. I can't help it. That's just looks. *Superficial.*

Who would have wanted to murder me? Who would want to now? I am a maimed mythological figure—statue—alone in a motel. This is the moreor-less truth of me and I don't mean Medea.

I am living in the Palms Motel, telling my fortune. I am living in a tawdry heap of boards called the Palms Motel.

———

The body was discovered before my eyes. I stood there awhile surveying the death which was mine. Why doesn't anyone understand that I own it? My murderer doesn't, even though I'm in pieces like this: the artifice of the Iranian-type head and the more-like-Greek torso. Also, there's my heart there. Alongside, in Dead. The color red is around me.

So I had been murdered again. What else is new except some words? Dead is full of "again"s. How many times has it been? How can I connect with each murder? If you look at that shade of red, it becomes more intense, talking to you, making the assumption of connection: *I'm your blood.*

In Day even hummingbirds vibrate in unchanging colors. If you write in Day you are bound to colors. As if they were fixed. Whereas in Dead events seem sometimes to refer to the fixed, to the assumptions of Day, but you can pass through so much here so quickly, in all your bodies alive and defunct. Where else would you start to drown and suddenly be in a new body? Where else would you see the meagerness of your own expression as a corpse? Where else might you be a torso, beating at your own window?

Of course there are other colors than red in Dead, but it's often too dark to see them. Or just too weird. In Dead you're sometimes incomplete in presentation—hey, your body's melting! You're not interested in color in that situation. In Day you can't pull away from the continuity of colors, giving you a sense of completeness: they call that time. It leads to identity.

I write from Dead and all I'm sure of is that I continue, no matter what body I'm in. I am I perceiving, even if what I perceive is, according to the rules of Day, unfixed. Life here is hard to describe, and I am always looking for other, would I have to say, language?

Medea is a ghoul who describes nature to us, or to me, truly. Because she understands magic. She belongs to Dead; Dido does too, whose doings I will also refer to. They are both founders of our human fantasy. Maat, the Egyptian, by judging me amuses me. I think nothing whatsoever of their husbands/fathers and may never name them. Unless they show up in Dead to bother us.

I'm writing this as if I were inventing it, but it keeps getting truer and truer. I the murdered in Dead have no interest now in what anyone else has written. I'm not in touch and have no intention of touching.

In Dead form changes, genre changes. The reality is that it can't be kept track of. I watched myself be cut up. The body was discovered before my eyes. Then Dark Ray stood near my corpse. The Coroner. After that I was literally a new form.

The Indians. But I could be saying the Medes, the Etruscans, the Carthaginians, etc, except that in Day the Indians are alive. The Indians' task in Day is to rejuvenate their cultures via gambling since Fortuna has been so unkind to them. In Dead Dido may lecture to them on Fortune or Fate, but probably not in her own language. Would it be Latin or English? What would she lecture on in Phoenician? What would they say back in their languages, so many of which have disappeared? But maybe not in Dead. In Day one is only a Theory of Man; the Indians' languages are buried in boxes beneath the people's casinos. In Dead everything may be alive after all.

Medea though ghoulish is magical and rests on the point of all transformation so beware: you can't hold on near her, that's why she is so reviled.

—

All the documentation of the death by poison dress would tend to make you believe in death by poison dress. The authors—Euripides, Ovid—believe in it so profoundly one accepts the event and almost doesn't ask, Can I learn to do this too? I, myself, don't want to kill anyone but I'm interested in how this process unfolds as I poison the pages you're reading. I don't want you to burn up and die like Creusa: I want you to understand I can affect your physical process by writing. I'm not contradicting what I previously said: I'm not going to touch you. My hands don't stick out of the page; and I don't want to make you cry. I want to demonstrate that this—the world we live in—is imagined, and transmutable in more ways than we are used to discussing.

Why kill anyone? There are much more radical things to do.

I need to write in verse for a moment
effecting a temporary change. Can you
feel it? I'd always rather write a poem.
But I'm shaky, lacking in control. The murder
makes me nervous, this talk of my own death. No,
it's more that I'm afraid prose won't go deep enough.
It can't solve the murder this time; because it didn't pose
it, the deathly situation, in the first place
Poetry tells me I'm dead; prose pretends I'm not.

And yet I go on in prose.

In Dead, voices have begun to speak to me in old languages: it sounded like Latin last time. In English a man's voice said, "The prisons are fragile." All the prisons at this time *are* fragile, that is, the prisons of form. He said as well, "Move on," but I translate that as Use the fragility for change.

Solve my murder or perhaps the murder of Creusa, you ask?

Dark Ray: I a professional suggest that Creusa's murder was solved thousands of years ago. And I don't believe that you're dead. You always rejuvenate after I've dissected you.

I: But we don't know that Creusa was murdered. . . You must learn to read more of the languages inside me, not just English. There's something on my liver. I don't think it's old Iranian but rather a form of hybrid poetry, that you could decipher if anyone could. I've often resorted to new forms of expression; in Dead they all call to me as if neglected. Each like a ghoul, an experiential equation, alive only to remember itself. Head, torso, love, a certain shape of column of words.

Perplexing, Dark Ray says, a coroner whose job is to read the inside of my body.

If I wrote down that
there's a lot of love in me,
Medea would pack up

and leave. You must
understand we can't
do love, she'd say. It's

too late. Think of me as
a dead language. (Alive!)
What of the murder?

Where's the corpse?

From coroner's report (inner text):

This very beautiful body, in the heart of the old language
beneath the black seams of her spirit, pockets
of Latin-like words: and baccili to be analyzed,
squirming. She is: head with feminized hair under
argentine rotted headress, as prev. mentioned, with words around
face (skull) in script (French-style handwriting): **cosa**
matissus: *meaningless. The torso separate (head severed)*
the heart removed but left near. Legs are bones.
The heart
        onyx-covered
the heart sliced open with rock-cutter showing that
it is black and weighty. Are we speaking of myself.
I could propose many other bodies of mine, but to continue—
words within her torso everywhere on all organs
but covering the liver most densely and over each other
so it is difficult to discern the language(s) much less what
they say.

The suggestion is that all bodies are full of words, in fact. This particular
coroner, Dark Ray, can see some of it; writes double reports, one "normal,"
one for a "ghoulish" club who relish such morbid text. There is a murder

plot involving a club member who kills to provide the coroner with bodies for the club's eventual reading activities. He especially likes to murder me.

Below the box below the Casino lies the Black Sea. Which has by now infected all my seams.

—

When I eat the blood-sac, I think of Judgment, whom I'm loathe to call on. She makes the atmosphere pompous, up to the point where she might eat me, *her* blood-sac, as it were; she must go on too. Even a goddess has to survive, even if she were the goddess of compassion or other soft rot, for there's a lot of old rot in this story of ghouls.

Dark Ray: I found a transcription within the corpse of a meeting between her and Judgment—Maat.

Ghoulish Club Member: If I devour these words myself, they may protect me from adverse judgment.

Dark Ray: Better than a blood-sac?

Ghoulish Club Member: A blood-sac is just more blood. Let's see some transcript here.

FROM TRANSCRIPT:

'I found you in a precise room within by calling out to you. I need you to find me and tell me what I've done.'

'How can I identify what exists as social phantasm? even with the crown of thorns you wear.'

'My cultural headress?'

'You kept trying to go past it.'

'But I don't know if I believe it. If there really is a weight of passion . . . On the highway there's no one to tell me if I've gone wrong, so I've picked you.'

'Is it important that you have a weight of passion?'

'It's important that I have my own weight. Why has this life been so serious? Do I have to explain it to you, as if you weren't only another such

one? How can I be judged if I don't care about my past? I only doubt
it—mere story, though don't doubt its weight.'
'I'm not weighing stories only your heart. Nothing
      you tell me
      can change your heart's
      weight. You are the
      creature
      of its weight.'
'Do you really have the right to weigh my heart?'
'My own heart is heavy.

            If I
            weighed my
            heart against
            my own

            feather
            I'd stand
            condemned

            You must
            never
            tell

            as I learned
            from the other
            gods, never tell

            where you've been.

            I am a
            part of your
            being

            from before
            your
            birth; you and I

know each
other so
well we don't have to

almost
don't have to
do this.'

'In all my automatic parts—as in calling to you—there is an element I
would have called lies before. I know that I am speaking to you now. What
have I done with my life? Is that question the weight of my heart?'

'It doesn't have to be unless it takes the weight. I've brought my scale, at
your call. I'm tempted to throw the scale away. But, put your heart on the
scale—'

'It's there . . .'

'This feather
is a lie. But

it covers you,
for your heart is as

light as my feather.'
'How can that be?'

'Your heart is judged
weightless, by me

I am Judgment
the goddess of this moment

which weighs nothing.
                    Above
I float spread my arms out over

your horizon—what else would
I do? I came to balance you;

You are free from Judgment.
Your heart is a feather, replace it

within you. Continue.'

Dark Ray: It isn't fair, I'd say. Who could believe this anyway?
Ghoulish Club Member: Swallow it; I'd swallow it.
Dark Ray: I have to be a scientist in order to keep cutting her open; I can't go off into myth. But I need to know where she's been—the murders are so necessary.
Club Member: What would you do without me?

———

Dido: The purpose, even goal, of Fortuna is to render those it favors unknowingly stupid: it—she—whatever—is saying, you are so stupid you think you're rewarded for your national goodheartedness, your democratic airs; or your personal intelligence. God's gift. You are not rewarded at all; you eventually die into a pile of shit. For her amusement. History seems oblivious to the irony that, thus, only mouth-breathers (people too dumb to inhale through their noses) succeed. People who think they are more than future fertilizers. A reading of history demonstrates that the Americans, the British, ancient Romans and Greeks, many others, are thus cretins.
Especially the ancient Greeks, Medea confirms.
I: As the destroyed cultures seep into my consciousness, air of the Black Sea, claiming me in Dead. Women have always been in Dead, ghouls dreaming a poisonous vengeance, supposedly on each other (story of Creusa), but I am trying with every syllable to infect the Coroner's club and also make my way around the maddening dark Business Suit often blocking my way, the suit of Dark Ray.
Dido: When Medea and her not-to-be-named Greek lover—man of no depth whatsoever (how was *she* so dumb?)—left the Black Sea for Greece (did this really happen), he and the Argonauts helped engender the Casino—business. Vote management, female and "minority" management: keep them calm while counting the votes of free Greek men. Keep them

calm while counting. Cash, but also the "kinds of life" observable in Day. Ownership of shapes, of species. Invention and maintenance of borders: count those countries, so you can take them over. Don't let ambiguity infect your mind. Mind? Fortuna says, You have no mind; I've proven that by seducing you in my sometime-did-me-seek, off-the-shoulder garb.

I'm sorry if you don't get all the allusions. You dumb ghouls.

I: I'm a ghoul, Medea's a ghoul, Dido's a ghoul, the club member's a ghoul, Dark Ray is too: we all swallow red to go on. Descendants of lost cultures—do you really think women don't automatically belong to one of those? The club member, male, is also historically descended from slaves (I won't say which slaves, there have been so many in history) and is propelled by the urge—oh these Latin-rooted words—to free himself though he's *free*. He knows, just knows, that if he could read the inside of my body—bodies—his manumission would be complete. Why? Because I'm a *writer*, a truthteller and prophet. This is perhaps outmoded, but he is old, a ghoul. He will swallow blood-sac after blood-sac until he is free, that is to say, *alive*. Alive again. Then it may be possible to die.

I am a ghoul, and I preserve my remains by living. I too have to find things out. I don't kill, I am killed. In rhythm to what it is presumed I have found out.

As for Medea, Medea should never have left the Black Sea, she says.

It was literally black then. I am Medea and I have never been pathetic, as portrayed by Chaucer. I have transformed my own history by swallowing enough blood to have lived so long as to have rewritten every word within me. Being the sorceress who changes history all the way backwards. You think I did everything with herbs, having been trained on the banks of the Black Sea? Herbs?

The Poet may have listed the names of plants, in script or oral tradition, as if by his lists he could imagine me, but he knew nothing of me or of the original Black Sea. All of my power comes from the original Black Sea. All of Dead with its red dots of blood-sacs for Going On. One will try to control me again by putting me in regular meter or justified prose, but I will say a different shape that flows. Dark as the opals red-specked he'll try to give me: Fortuna will bless him again so that in his nightmare brain he wins. Any known he. In Dead they are worthless. Why the successful never sleep. You are so clumsy in your dreams, my love. But in Dreams Medea has the power not just of names but of seams: I can flow easily when your legs fail.

Because you counted your parts, you idiot, and so made your legs be
separate from you.

———

Anyone might inhabit borderless ghoul air
Dido continuously founds Carthage there
as writers try to control her, placing her on her pyre
she cuts up the bull's hide enclosing the future
citadel, called Hide. (*Around this fort Carthage rose.*)
I was in flames. They were lines. It was a drawing
Trembles emotively? This was no location of self-hatred
I was in flames, but they were straight lines, drawn by
me, burning up; I founded a city. *He* founded
the city which destroyed mine entirely: have you
ever read a Carthaginian poem? With ghouls
I'll found this city, until our poems are obvious
confirming the magical nature of our human
art: in straight lines myself a girl burning
I was in flames, presaging thousands of corpses
'What is it to lose your country, a great suffering?'
Lost it once before I came here; again after I died
when the Romans extirpated 'our race': as if we were any
repulsive people in any modernity; needed our blood
Do you need it too? (My name was really Elissa.)

———

Dark Ray says he has to know what I know. Why does he have to know
this? He isn't clear. Partly he needs to make sure I don't know too much,
more than him, about anything he knows, because if I know what he knows
as well as what I know, I'm superior. On the other hand what I know—
should know—is only what a woman knows and though that may be

considerable knowledge, it's only known by a woman . . . As long as it doesn't become operative. But then again, what if I *know*? The truth is, he and his club are hooked on me, there's no other way to put it.

The transcriptions from inside your corpses are upsetting him, Medea says. You seem to know everything by now. What if you do become operative? After all, my job is to make you so.

I will probably soon become a corpse again, in my room at the Palms Motel. I will escape that corpse and eat another blood-sac.

The Ghoulish Club Member is trying to stay alive long enough to know enough. Why can't he know it on his own? Can only read; I am like his most precious blood-sac. And what or who is my own most reliable blood-sac, someone might ask? I'm not clear on this matter. Suddenly I am eating a literal sac of blood; I become reddish, the color of my hair and my lips changes. Reddens. What am I swallowing, Medea? Do you know?

Eat it, she says. It's knowledge. From dead cultures. It's also blood.

Elissa. Should I call her Elissa or Dido? (For years I myself have been told my name was actually my husband's name, one or another of them.) I think the Romans renamed her Dido: a culture is the same as a husband. Her people had traveled from Phoenicia to settle in Africa. Where I recently passed through Judgment, encountering Maat, in another country. When Dark Ray read of this, in my corpse, he was furious. He hates the non-regular nature of Dead. He just knows ancient countries can't arise and dissolve like that. They are stationary, dissectable like bodies. They died of discernable causes: poor health or, more rarely, murder. Accidents (marvelous Latin word) like being in the way of an empire's velocity. They can't have a life after death.

It was a most beautiful torso—my last corpse, marble with traces of paint: in the Afghani manner more Alexandrian Greek than Buddhist, the sort of cultural mix that art critics can disdain for its lack of purity—which is perceived as lack of originating genius and of intensity.

But how did an exotic, broken statue come to be at a shabby motel?

Inside me will be further poems and texts. I am working on them now. Will they be poisonous to the coroner, Medea?

Beauty's often poisonous.

The Palms Motel has an old blue linoleum floor, blue background, with a lighter pink-shaded floral pattern against the blue. All of that flickers and darkens since this is Dead. I find the floor beautiful.

Has Dark Ray read my palms? Was I fortunate? Oh I had no palms, it was mostly a torso. My last hands are in another country, but any proper conqueror-scientist could find them.

A serious historian was present at the crime scene. Says: Can you tell if it's a buddha or a woman? Because if it's just a woman . . .

Official in some bureau tries to convince you your name is your husband's. You were married weren't you? This is a poem I'm not bothering to set in line breaks. It's raining outside, don't do anything dumb, official says, don't try to change your civil state. Which must of course be my husband. Official's brown-skinned and from a colony. Originally. Originally . . .

How many times have they changed your name in which countries.

Don't be pathetic, Medea says, like Elissa/Dido.

How many blood-sacs has she eaten in order to keep trying to found a city in Dead?

—

Colors . . . Creusa . . . seen. That was for awhile.

Now I can't be. Changed the terms of my existence. *Before your eyes.* So I can't be.

They wanted to see it in me, what they put there.

Certain that their instruction would be received. Having seen the true advantage of the story of Creusa burning in a dress. You did it, they could say to me, Medea. Or that the children . . .

To give me the guilt that would freeze my actions. Or make me despised (I am that—despised or pitied.) So that I would stand to the side.

Creusa: not a lead part though she suffers. *I'm* offended—yes—that she can't be a lead. I have no interest in dramatic hierarchy, though no one can believe that whatever the age. I stand for a fiery truth that every being is a lead. How else talk to a bird? a plant? if it isn't a lead. You can't even let Creusa fill up her own death.

And then suddenly that damned implanted image cluster was inside me. It had probably been the Greeks. I can't extract it the butcher said. Not so far from where I began. But probably much later than when I'd begun. It's always like that.

I'd asked him to remove it. Form of brain surgery. Have never wanted anyone else's thoughts and feelings to be mine. What would you have if you didn't have those, Medea, the butcher said? He thought you start out empty.

With the mind, with existing, does it even start? Does a two-millimeter-tall *man* click it on?

They were trying to set up their action in my mind, way back then in ancient now. A Greekish blonde woman slipped it in before I could know. I began to wait to see it happen, to have to deal with it. Hallucinations. The blonde hovered. I'm messing with your head. Why? So you can see a story. All of us want you to see it. How are you doing this? Magic.

Then out in the hypermarket I see it though it doesn't blot out the whole other one: it's their Creusa story playing in the middle of shopping for food.

I see what they said, the *robe* and she's burning; I didn't do that: Yes you did the blonde says it's in your memory now, it's in your psyche. Greek word. And now we all know. Know it and know what you did. This is your internal corona, she says. She's low forehead, bossy without much intellect. How does she know about magic? It's wherever *anyone* finds it.

So I go to the butcher. Suggest surgery to get out these tumorous *ideas* that are the *people's* pleasure (oh *fuck* the people): You did it, didn't you. You're like that, aren't you. If I say no . . . Because I thought it was a *thing*.

My mind's too textured for this crappy story: do you know the language of the thrush? I do. Above you I have seen. Sometimes I can understand all language.

You understand too much, they said. We must drive you mad, before you change everything. MEDEA, YOU'RE A MURDERER!

So what did I do about this, use my magic? It depends on what you think that is. I pushed the story out of my mind.

I'm a technician, aren't I? No how did I get it out? I made my mind hard (a specialty) and pushed the implant out of my head. It still existed in everyone else's head, it *still* exists in the world . . . The story, the lies about me. Images, that you'll always believe. That I poisoned another woman, killed my brother and my own children. The purpose of the story: to establish as reality, that a woman of power can only be evil. This phenomenon has been truly magical.

We want you, Medea, to be the worst thing that there is.

I make my mind as ancient as I can: to expel you. You the story, still alive a larval slime. A grim little being they love so. Here's the expelled story in my hand, writhing pus.

Do you believe one thing about yourself, I'd ask all of you—you the world—but you'd say yes. I'd say, there's nothing in your reality but random stories.

If you want to kill something, kill that story of me. No, you love it too much.

Flames everywhere in front of me; but they aren't a story. They're an example of who I talk to, because you can talk to anything, and if your mind isn't full of implanted stories, anything might talk back. The guild of scientific personages will call that projection; I don't work with them.

The flames have to be burning something, you say, how destructive you are, Medea.

They're burning all my old thoughts.

You've done this before.

I do it over and over. I have to in order to continue. To be this ghoul I am.

—

Whose flames are we? We're us, our own. Are we more than one fire? I'm my own flame. Talk to Medea, Dido.

Dido is burning. Founding.

Her people burned babies to the gods. Later. They did that after she died. Isn't dead. She was never dead.

She's a fiction. She burned nothing. Nero burned Rome. She killed herself burning.

They discovered vases of babies' ashes within Carthage, the archaeological site.

We're not like that.

There is no Dido.

Dido is a poem who has permeated you; one you can read within people who never read it.

She didn't found Carthage. She was abandoned by a lover. What did she do really?

If she founded Carthage, it was on the blood of babies.

Founders who are women only burn.

Dark Ray, in his Dark suit, his dark tie, stands in his coroner's office, trying to read the new corpse. Why does it speak of burning? It didn't burn.

Send your children to war; they can burn up foreign cities.

Dido: I'm a multitude of flames of cultures.

Dark Ray peers at the text in my corpse: murdered again, just a few Dead nights ago.

I was sitting in the Palms Motel, my feet on the linoleum floor, looking at books.

This is a photograph of pieces of Afghani antiquities. They were broken to be sold on the black market. Read the photo in me, my corpse says. Heads of buddhas, truncated thoughts. Each the same and different: pointed topknot, rounder topknot, long earlobes, longer earlobes. Does that face look more serene than that one?

I AM A BROKEN CULTURE!

No, I'm burning.

No, I'm founding a culture for you the fire.

Medea: The flames of course say *I am pure*. Red lines which spread out tissue-like.

In the city of ghouls I must found something substantial. In the culture of ghouls.

Why is Dark Ray wearing such clothes? The Coroner pretends to mourn for me. He's trying to get the story, reading and reading.

It's a new corpse, recently found in a trunk. Her face peeled off and glued back on her skull, a smile cut into her flesh. Pool of blood around the trunk. Is it me? Of course.

I'm sitting in the Palms Motel. I've been reborn, you sucker. I look rather like a statue again.

Dark Ray: I've got to keep something for my death, my real death when it comes. What can I keep? I know it's here in this text. It's got to be here this time.

You're not supposed to keep something for yourself; you're supposed to found a city.

Are you?

When Dido crawled onto her pyre, she cursed the man who'd abandoned her. After the Romans burnt Carthage, they said a curse against any who would refound the city.

In my story, who is cursed? It depends on what city's being founded. It isn't Carthage after all, but the city of ghouls.

If Dido and Medea have been abandoned by their lovers, they will never mention it here. They don't care any more.

I have endured. Why?

Why do you keep talking about Medea and Dido? Dark Ray asks. Why don't you give me something, something to keep?

———

Proceed with greatest delicacy, the text inside the new corpse says.

The region is rich, it is true, in relics; and coins of every sort show almost straight through the soil . . . Persian, Parthian, Sassanid medals are no less common . . .

Does it really matter where I was? I always wanted to get beyond, before then. Now that I've been around so long, am a ghoul, I don't care much. I pursue the thought as a reflex.

When I was traumatized in my sex and ceased to mate with anyone. For you will understand severe breakage of a work or cultural entity results in myriad heads stolen, small masks that might be dug up *only*—no temples or grand monuments. And as I was repeatedly broken and possessed by scholar-archaeologists as well as starving natives and conquering soldiers. After the love loss. Those are inconclusive sentences, as you are an invader too, my coroner.

There was a fire somewhere, I remember. People jumped from a roof. My poems were up there in boxes; my poems were burned in the fire. Or am I seeing the future?

That isn't about sex, Dark Ray says to my text within. Why does your thought wander so?

He needs words to claim. For what purpose but cultural: personal, general, both. What does he really want? A form of self-justification. Thus he breaks my form repeatedly. To understand it, have it, destroying everything but himself. Ah, sorry, I've accidentally broken your culture! Will there be an intact statue left anywhere?

My manuscripts are lost our language
forgotten
who'll know the letters people fall from the burning
loft where my manuscripts
were stored
my poems are gone

This isn't about sex! Dark Ray screams into the corpse. You said you were traumatized in your sex. Why don't you stay on the subject?

The Ghoulish Club Member, the murderer, has entered and says, I put a dress on her. I bolted it to her skin, to go with the mask I made of her face this time.

It's hard to say, about sex, my text continues. And, I am going further back. Many things the same.

The hands of new warriors are pushing up through the ground. They're always growing somewhere.

Again, proceed with delicacy. I was precisely abandoned, but the death of a lover freezes the statue, that is, body. I know you thought the statue was a form, the shape of a work, that any one—man—might earn or own. The statue was also my remains as sex the flower states whose color is probably red; but we are seeing obscurely in this region of Dead which evidently shifts. Because I don't want to tell any more. If someone's gone, you stay at home.

It's cold for me on this cooling board, and I don't like the mask my body's forced to wear.

An important production of small masks—which often bear a suspension ring—characterizes the Punic world, these works, seeming by their technique to be jewelry, have without doubt a magic value . . . and were considered to be talismans protective against evil forces.

He wants me to protect him. By being dead and carved by him, I'm a fetish against evil. Evil to him is his real annihilation. He's afraid to die, as a ghoul can, finally, die. We don't talk about that much in Dead.

Who shocked you so? Should say 'what.' What shocked you, love? Death shocked me, not mine though. And so have no more sexual visions, who knows if I miss them? busy to die again, be read.

Other women, torsos, broken in war. The conquerors pick them up, put them in sturdy sacks and leave. . . As far back as I can recall.

—

Dark Ray: I'm drawn to her in all her corpses but I don't know what to do with her. Do I prefer her cut up in cultural fragments, or smiling from the Club Member's incisions? My own incisions are gentler.

I can't die without knowing what she knows, but I know she can't really know anything. One must arrive at the point of actual death having evinced more scientific rigor than she's capable of. In whatever one's studies. Because. Though I'll be dead. And I won't know I'm dead. Will I? I've only died once or twice, but really to die . . . But Really to Die.

Ghoulish Club Member thinks: Does Judgment know about me? She *must* approve of my murders—Because they're mine. Everyone knows that whatever's really theirs is more than acceptable.

I:

I understand who I was: the dream of the foreigner.
Composed of parts of your show
I, I thinking this thought, is it mine? You have
to love, for it's apparent you do. And even ghouls
hundreds of us somewhere like center of a city.
Or Motel to be alone in. Anywhere else one's a martyr
to these ghoulish features of continuance. *He* was
hung up for meat, marked for carving, too.
'It's the only way to stay alive.' She looked at the
butcher through her glasses demanding her husband.
Ghoul, said the butcher, don't you know what he
was for? To serve the species; go on on your own
If you can keep your parts together, you'll get some-
thing. What will I get? I can't tell you.

I don't know if it's "can't" or "won't." Who the hell wants to serve this species?

I call to Medea most seriously to prove a more magical point. *My* point: that one must find a way to be her; and has not been allowed to for all of our history, thus the claptrap of the murders she's supposed to have committed when the real murder goes on all night. Who is being murdered if not I?

I want to hear something. Something between the words. Something from somewhere else. Some truthful music.

Case a tear wood. I heard the sounds of that. 'Tear' sounds like 'tier.' Neither 'case' nor 'wood' need necessarily be spelled that way. Case a tear wood.

The Coroner stands in his bulk radiating his dark suit. Monomaniacal, cut and read, cut and read, until he knows everything as material standard decided by whoever says the evidence is mounting. So why is he so frightened? The evidence is never conclusive. I'm not there; I've escaped again leaving poetry.

Bring me her corpse he says.

I just did that the Club Member says.

I didn't like the expression on her face, Dark Ray says, it was counter to the complexity in her ... her ... what are these bodies? Are they like errands she assumes? Anyone assumes?

You do it this time, the Club Member says. You murder her. I can't do it again. I need a break from this bloodshed.

—

They keep saying that she loved too hard; it's what they know how to say. (Did I love too hard?) In order to speak of a life. For example, to see a poet that way is easier than reading her poems, especially long ones (but when will I ever be dead enough for this to happen?) Leave me alone, no read me.

Medea: I can't even remember her, Creusa. Did I meet her? But the children, procuring food for them each day, cleaning their baby bodies behind the foreign buildings on my own, for everyone suspects a skillful woman whose possessions are diminished for whatever reason.

To be me. That is to know the language, a golden inscription felt under the skin. It, the language, trembles, not fixed, in Dead. And no it's not the names of kings or gods:

*In the beginning there was inquiry: can change to enmity or enemy, your job, poet, is to hold it on inquiry long enough for a note of the choir—*inquiry*—to transfer the letters to sound which liquifies the statue/body so it moves. This is moving. This text is always changing. What alphabet doesn't matter, which language. It's mine.*

I'm sitting, I, in the Palms Motel, attempting to read my palms, before I am murdered again. I believe Dark Ray may engender my demise this time. I seem to see into his mind, for he walks about fearfully. Does this move me? I wonder if anything does. There is an M in my palm but it stands for Medea not Me. Symmetrical, the same going forwards or backwards; some say the citizens of Corinth stoned her children in their grief for Creusa. More lies.

YOU MUST STOP MURDERING ME.

Medea: They implanted their words in me and implanted lies about me in everyone! I've stayed alive this long in order to see the story recanted, burned. As you do that for me—change my story, I teach you my arts. And we found for all ghouls a ghoulopolis, I suppose.

The Palms Motel is our first edifice. This tawdry place. Though it is a local landmark on account of its age. Built on a ramshackle base but never breaks down. Several palm trees outside. The neon still comes on, spells "Palms Motel" in green script.

Page: ". . . and finally a sort of death-wish denial that the key to proper understanding can ever be recovered"—key to the first texts within, beyond Carian, Luvian, Linear B. Or cuneiform. Or middle European signs. I'm not reading *palms* anymore.

You can of course read your own body, Medea says, better than any self-importantly, black-clad, doomed Coroner can. You read it whenever you move, or don't, you statue! You look somewhat Etruscan now. Long nosed and smiley.

She continues, I am already showing you the interfaces between Dead and Day. I know a rigor that no one alive remembers; *you* know it without awareness of it. Our city full of echoes and broken things; our city stripped of its plaques of inscription and celebration; our city of all souls, inter-preted as ghouls, is in each's own body. Dido, can you hear me?

Who is Medea if she isn't what I do now? But I keep acting like a statue.

Dammit I'm still trying to tell my fortune after millennia. Will I make it, to what? I want something else to happen—more than vindication for Medea. So I stare at my palm, which hasn't changed since, 3000, 5000 BC. Why can't the human change? Then I play poker on a hand-held machine: my version of the Casino. Playing poker by myself. Somewhere in between the palm and the poker I talk to Indians: do you care if I call you Indians?

We don't bother about you, they say.

Your casino's the loudest one I've been in, I say. Loud music that no one ever moves to.

We can't bear the silence of the night, this era.

No one can stand it, but at least it isn't my palm. If I stare at it it starts humming a backwards hum, that is, it tells me the trouble with my fortune is that it all lies in the past. Everything I did, but also everything I don't know. What is a human, I mean ghoul—is the answer in the past or in the future?

What do you think, Indians?

You know we think we know—knew—but we were conquered. The human truth is eradicated, by coins in slots, blackjack, money games.

You have a school and a power plant.

In Day. But in Dead, the pieces are windblown and where whites drift along the water, everything we knew made insecure is present but partial; all the Ghouls trail coins they don't care for. Coins are the archaeologists' love, and the love of the short-sleeved, smoking old, pushing buttons in order to go on. No one cares about any of it except to go on.

Dark Ray is part Indian. That's another piece or part. But Dido and Medea are part of his heritage burning. I am part of all of them. But I know I can only see right now. Look, it's ugly!

The M in my palm, Medea leaps out shrieking:

The original Black Sea was really full of black water. It looked almost like fizzy cola when the waters rose. The ship I was in contained me. Well it had some sailors—ghouls now—and so I see ghouls aboard; there was no Jason (there I've said the name), because there is no Jason here now. This is to be precise and change reality. We were seeing what was there. Scattered bones ashore. BUT. You will notice the one consistency in all the stories of myself is that my end is deferred. The only truth of me. Now backwards into the future the ship goes . . .

Dark Ray: I must defend myself before *she* kills me. I believe she is killing—trying to kill—my modernity. Whatever she may say in the manner of pacifism. I think I need to kill her in the final way; this sort of pursuit of 'truth' goes nowhere. I want a life in Day, interaction with *people* not ghouls. That's what the truth's about: the human situation of grave crises in the background, everyone doing something in relation to blood flowing; the problem of money, money as problem (i.e. necessity); the atmosphere of the quest among *contemporary* gestures and figures. Doesn't that sound like freedom? I could fall in love. But I don't understand if it's *she* I should kill or Medea.

I: I'm sitting in the Palms Motel. It is an enclave within myself. Outside the ghouls sing in famine, for famine penetrates into Dead. You can only sympathize with such urgency yourself— if you're not hungry—when the borders between bodies are down. Why you (the reader) like to wake up, but I never wake up. The hungry, who are or will be the conquered (conquered by both those who withhold food and those who feed them) have the dignity of starvation; their ghoul-souls are quiet in the extremity of their fatigue.

Will blood-sacs be given out tonight? But I don't even know how I get mine. There are so many more ghouls than before, dying, dying again, for the conquerors.

The commanders regret life's brevity for themselves their parent beard
they are the class thousand wars to whom only comes the elusive spring
came not to me magician though I broke the gods of their procuration
startled the common places ripped to bear up their navy or oral possession
they neither rule me nor sequester my bitterest regnum of itinerant fact
I arrived to make fold of auric tendancy in the atmospheric transverse
unturned to necessitate honesty's pay while they cynically bade us
address a plaint to feigned arbitration assemble and expend in invention
primarily to please the fleet not the deep, oh fasten up smoothly
your accessible beauty its unnecessary and illimitable mode
you are the conquerors paying no one, being vantage's own surly breath
being the simplest invective mantled in the letters of victorious lead.

Meeting of the Club. This is an anxious ancient group who love to seem knowledgeable. They are in Control of their Club, but they are afraid of having done to them what they do to others.

So I have to kill her next time, Dark Ray says. Ghoulish Club Member number one now refuses.

We need some new literature desperately, says Member. We haven't had text in days.

You mean sext, says Member.

There is of course one woman Member who now says, Objtextion. In Dead, for in Dead, for in Dead whatever transpires is only almost funny, only almost makes sense.

They're forgetting me for a minute, Dark Ray thinks. No one can forget about me even a minute. I'm thinking of trying to finalize her death, he announces in a louder voice.

Do we know how? says Member.

It isn't possible in Dead, says Member.

Nothing can die in Dead, says Member, since one's already dead. Except for when it finally just happens.

I'm thinking of eradicating all textual possibility within her. If I could stop her body from writing she would be dead. She only lives to write. Isn't that so?

We need her words, I personally crave them, says Member.

We can get words from the others. Someone will replace her as favorite corpse, Dark Ray says. She's driving me crazy, he glowers. Her words attack us; her body comes to pieces in a minute as if she were waiting to be read. I'm bored with her torso. I found a new word in her last transcript: *genofest*. A combo of genocide and festival. It applies to us. We, by killing her over and over—granted she has a lot of bodies—are celebrating a genofest.

Insult, Member says.

It should have been *genocifest*, Member says.

But we do kill her and others repeatedly, Member says.

All Members look thoughtful.

Are we really conquerors? says Member.

We conquer people because they need it, another says. So they can be read, broken into pieces, and distributed to the true appreciators of their forms. They can't do this by themselves.

We liberate her each time she dies, Member says.

Get to point. How will you eradicate all text within her? asks Member.

Dark Ray says, I will destroy her base ghoul.

Ahh! They all say.

There is an ancient potion, says Dark Ray, that eradicates a ghoul. We haven't ever used it before; we scarcely know how we finally die in Dead. Let's find out!

Dido is haunting the Club, lurking in a corner, behind some damaged art. Thinks, They are so like the Romans and Greeks, solemn little men.

Member says, What if she's becoming Medea? Medea never dies . . . I know this as a classics major. (Member is getting off on role here.) I don't think you can kill Medea that way.

Dark Ray glowers again (he thinks the word as he does it). It hasn't happened yet. There's still time; she hasn't learned all of the Medean arts.

Dido: Though they think like cartoons, they are often effective. It's because they're always allowed to do as they please. But all the genocide victims throughout history are amassing in our city. I am founding it truly. Though I don't understand what it's like.

Maat watches everything hovering above us with her wings of in Dead spread out, the feathers refusing to resolve into either blue or green. I'm tired of my jobs, she's thinking. I'm tired of hovering, I'm tired of judging, I'm tired of maintaining the appearance of balance. And if I'm tired, something big is going to happen here in Dead.

Affixing crisis into changeable Dead isn't easy
                                        Perhaps
chaos expands until the back of Dead breaks
until the dorsal skin splits, its spine revealed.

Whose spine's cut open so you can watch my
figure playing keyboard—gaps open between
the keys, until we're just learning to think again.

Staring at my palms I've begun to see.

The lines connecting my hands and spine
are a gold-black current, Medea
My back tells me to play the keys but
these words emerge: *You don't know us*
so play anything. How do you do that, Medea

To stand where nothing's formed,
how—this palmistry opens
first to M, then to noise. Nostalgia
breaks you, but chaos, No. M, N, O go
past on my way. Leaving them

At the métro station Q-K I'd almost
gone too far. E-qe or ekue means *Hear this*
in Minoan, don't you know? A warning not to
go further. I listen to my spine, not these social
stations. Medea, what can too far possibly be?

Foolish men afraid of *magic*
want it, of course. It's just beneath known letters
Sail back over the Black Sea, above
alphabet. A letter was once fishes
Or it was once a head. He put a man's cap on it, didn't he

I'm listening to the sounds in these palms.
The connections I've made to my Back.

Letter B comes before where you
are. The spine opens to further. It hears it
my senses organizing ghoulish novelty.

Magic, keep him from killing me.
After all this time. I'd like to say that he
hasn't the right, but I don't know
if that goes. There are no rights here.
Magic, I just ask you for me.

How do ghouls really die
I think they decide to, says one ghoul
I think they know they have to; but
it hasn't come to me yet, she says
I don't want to go now says the ghoul. I haven't

received what I'm owed.

⌒

    There are blood-sacs for the taking among the potsherds. Or is it a
cemetery? Feed me like the others. Is it real blood? The red of it goes grainy
and grey; the color crawls across the form. The statute is to go on doing
good; good begins with eating the blood-sac. I don't know how it continues.
    We are here in the graveyard, Medea, Dido, and I. Medea hands me a
blood-sac; Dido is draining hers. Her pale face takes on color. This is our
city, she says. Our foundation myth, she says, sarcastic.
    Are you from the famine, my love? Would I almost let you eat me? I'm
speaking to a ghoul.
    You are broken art, that ghoul says bitterly.
    I can't be perceived as edible.
    Eat your blood-sac, says Medea. I swallow some.

This carries us back, forward, she says. Back to the point where it started. Where blood-sacs were generated. Where we began to eat.

Some soldiers are shooting from the tombs. Over there. They're aiming across the street at half-wall buildings. They don't seem to have time to swallow blood.

Why protect ghouls in Dead? Dido asks. Force of habit, she answers herself. What's the difference between you and me, Medea?

What?

You're the I that refuses to comply. Or testify. I'm the lissome Elissa, the you in a man's eye. Only in his eye. But that's trite, we're just more eaters of blood-sacs.

Found a city on this, I say, why?

Because it's already here, says Medea. In the greater death rate of time as it is lived progressively, going forwards, more and more ghouls are generated. But each time we eat a blood-sac, we're back where we started to do that. I see a city arise on the banks of the Black Cauldron, over and over, cathedral, capitol, and battlefield. I can't accept a single one of those elements. Can I only defy it? And I stand there. On the banks of the Black Sea. Watching more and more forms emerge from its cauldron.

If all images are equal—and each one existing is thus as if created at the beginning—I must always be in the source of magic, I say.

The magic of Dead, Dido says.

Dark Ray approaches with a gun.

We run to hide behind headstones. Potsherds trip me but I manage to get down.

Dark Ray lurches between tombs. It's almost soothing to see him: a simple pursuit. Stay down, Dido says. We do.

Red was his hair. When. When did they get to have hair. Stop asking and eat your blood-sac, so your hair will grow thick and glossy.

We run away.

           ✧   ✧   ✧

Dark Ray gives up on the females, wonders again why he's in Dead not Day. He sits down and picks up a blood-sac. Where do they come from? No one's known where food comes from for eons.

Ghoulish Club Member number one finds him in his dejection, near some grave or other.

No one cares where blood-sacs come from, Dark Ray says. In Day there would be a vending machine or a restaurant. Something. A known source. He swallows some blood.

What do you think we're really up to? the Club Member asks. Why are we doing this?

I'm living in a metaphor I can't escape from. *She* would say life in Day is stupid too. You connect, you build, you multiply. You make more for glory. You are driven by urges inserted in you by Someone, or No one, depending on how you think. It all began when a cell divided etcetera.

And in Dead?

It's a flipped-over consciousness. Other side.

Where *should* we be?

I WANT TO BE IN DAY! Why bother, she'd say.

But maybe she's right. What do women get out of anything?

Dark Ray says, I don't know whose side you're on. I think you kill her too much.

I'm starting to know her too well, says the Ghoulish Club Member.

I am, Dark Ray says, going to go for the ultimate murder of her. Can you take it?

I don't know, the Ghoulish Club Member says.

They say genocide victims are amassing everywhere around here, millions of ghouls. More and more arrive every day. Will there be enough blood-sacs to go around? In Day I suppose they just disappear. The famine victims just die. The people in the wars just die and go away.

What about Medea? Dark Ray says. Can we do a routine kill on her, read her insides? I know it's never been done—she never even gets a superficial hit. Slips into air . . . But there must be a way. She may know how to kill someone in the final fashion. And she may know about a way out of Dead. First, why don't you try to kill Medea.

You *never* kill anyone, Club Member says.

Well I do have to cut them up, Dark Ray says hieratically. And I *will* kill *her*, but I have to find out how. To do it permanently.

Medea won't let me near.

Just try, Dark Ray says.

How did you catch Medea? I
found her standing at a crossroads
        staring
in a black cloak standing, staring
        at a red
flower. I'd lost this flower, she said
        and seemed
to welcome me. I'm not going to avoid
        my murderer
she said. Is this flower important? I

asked. He'll find out in my autopsy
        she said
when he cuts me up, that is if he
        can understand me.
I stabbed her and then picked the flower:
        it's blatant.
I feel like I'm in a story I can't follow.
I've always felt that way, no matter
        what. Here she
is, open her and read her: you're the
        coroner. Here she is.

How did you catch Medea? I
found her standing at a crossroads
        staring
in a black cloak standing, staring
        at a red
flower. I'd lost this flower, she said
        and seemed
to welcome me. I'm not going to avoid
        my murderer
she said.

I'm sitting in the Palms Motel, catching psychic flashes off my palms. Medea's on ice in the mortuary; the Coroner cuts her tomorrow. She told me they wanted to cut her to find the formula for my elimination. She said she didn't think she had it in particular. She knows few formulas; she does what she does out of air. They want her general knowledge: she says they won't find it.

Dido remains outside though they're after her too. She sits with the ghoulish, looking ghoulish; they have a maquette for a city. It's sometimes white and sometimes a bloody pink, the color changing as they look at it.

I'm in some mental channel where I hear Casino proprietors talking about the difference between a keyboard and computer poker controls.

You play a keyboard not knowing how it's going to sound: sits with his spine open showing the nerves, as he touches piano keys. 88 keys. What will happen? Who knows? And 52 cards, 5 buttons—nothing much happens; activity along spine? nothing much happens. You move your fingers, you ghoul—but the same thing changes. Rigid images. It's always the same thing changing, the proprietor mournfully says. We know all the changes.

She's taught me enough so I can stand by the black cauldron. She didn't really teach me anything, I got it by being around her. I stare at my palms then I seem to be there. A white webby shape emerges from time to time, hovers then goes. What will it be? A person or thing? An event? How does one move here? What's in charge?

Continuity is a mystery. It stumbles, stutters: the event of Medea's capture, for instance: the ghoul stabbed her beneath the breastbone, but then it was as if she forgot to bleed. Though she was lying dead, the next thing he knew. He screamed at her, You're not bleeding, and stabbed her again. Got a drop of blood.

The controls of Dead, say the proprietors, are like those of a worndown poker machine. You can't see the images of the cards very well; the machine never wears out though. Outside the river's thick and black. It's not very wide or very deep.

Dido asks if there has to be a casino in the future city. Everyone stops to think. They like the images on the cards but they don't like the games. They're old images, someone says. I'm an old image, Dido says. Am I worth retaining? Everyone stops to think.

How new can an old song be, played on the 88 keys? Pretty new.

Might be playing us high above Dead. Below Dead. Who's playing it? Sometimes one ghoul, sometimes another, is one thing to say.

———

Dark Ray's cut open Medea. Can he find what he wants?

Black Sea full of concubines, small plant-like. They give or take the implanted ring, scorches you though you never wear the bastard. The reason no one will ever understand me: I don't break. It's easy for you to read a fragmentary being, shaped conceptually by you. And oh god for a short while I tried to be a fragment. That means yours. Anyone's understanding of anything or one foreshortens it . . . Slipped away; I always got away.

Magic one steps into. They are too ignorant to know this moment and seize it . . .

Sometimes I'm in an ancient room and everyone I've disliked enters. Just comes in without calling or even knocking. It's all men and some girl students, women always students. How do I leave? It's my own room, isn't it? No. Dark Ray I'm poisoning you if you're here: the acidic feature is my intent to ruin your life. *She* would never do that, or wouldn't have before, but what I'm saying is the following: I'm poison. You're thoroughly wrong; you can't leave Dead; you're a ghoul. We're each a different kind of ghoul: the one you are is Wrong about Everything.

· · ·

What appears to me to be an anger inscription is coded into one symbol, an Etruscan A. I don't know how I know it's anger. I'm too upset to continue for awhile. Dark Ray says then shuts off the tape.

· · ·

The trouble with Jason was that he was silly. A liar. A believer in his *rights*. To be king! Great. One gets tangled up with these people. Now I want him to leave me alone, but he appears from time to time in hungry ghoul form.

So stuck. I refuse to remember anything else about him. I look at him; look away. He leaves.

POEM BY MEDEA

He comes for me; I don't go.

. . .

I stepped into a doorway in the dark. I realized I could be in My Version. The whole door vanished, I said, Let there be no light. There was already no light, but from that moment I started to shape the fact of no light.

There's poison where you touch me, Dark Ray, the poison of my not accepting Your Version. When I expelled the Creusa Etcetera implantation, there was a grooved carving left. I filled the grooves with a repellent, in case anyone tried it again. It's mental of course, but that's real. Don't touch it.

. . .

She doesn't seem to have any files, Dark Ray says into the mike. It's possible there's nothing left of her mind. After all this time. Her mid-section organs have a texture I haven't seen before. It could be print, but it's faint, worn. Covers everything. Experiential remnant?

And there's only a shadow in her skull—no actual brain. How does she think?

I can't bear it, Dark Ray says. There's no way for her to communicate with me, but I hear her. There's hardly anything to read, but I hear her voice. She isn't telling me anything so far, except that she's dangerous.

. . .

It's a poisonous love, not to give in. I'm slowly poisoning Your Version. I have no interest in your thoughts on any subject; though one sometimes listens to pass the time.

In My Version, that is Dead—which I don't own but do touch and interpret freely—one tinkers with time. If I don't have to take the time to listen to you, time changes. If you cease to schedule it, according to the way you want to run things—the 24 hour Casino/Coroner's Office/Club—you are, poor thing, shut out of your own times. Well you are, aren't you?

I have you in the dark, Dark Ray. I have you not knowing how things are run. Everything that should be here is here but in nightmare form; you see you're your own nightmare, don't you? Can you do anything about it if I don't let you?

But I only have so much control over what I'm doing. Also—this is important—it isn't clear to me what I want the world to be like. If I could change Dead, I'm not sure what I'd change it to. Dido has her maquette, but she toys with it aimlessly. She doesn't really know what to do.

. . .

Dark Ray throws the microphone down. He doesn't know who he wants to kill anymore. What does killing have to do with anything? He's beginning to wonder . . .

Are you in it yet, here, this magic
Nothing's in balance, you say. Or in key
Those phrases, events, don't work?
Maat's balance begs you do
something about your heart—If I
accept that, you, the reader, say,
I must be in it, what can I do with
it? *Your heart, fix it.* Your guilt
fix it. I stepped into a doorway and
the air, heavy with failure, changed
as if it now served a different machine
There is no machine. There's something
What story I reside in, who can prove?

I step into a doorway with a yellow light overhead. I don't try to enter the building; I stand with my back to the door. Where was I before? Probably at the Palms Motel.

I see a control panel in front of me flickering a moment. Made out of air. Gone. Over there you're sighing. But there's no you, it's only my breath.

I'd be a target for Dark Ray in this light. But I think I'm supposed to do this.

I could effect a change here, but I could effect a change anywhere, for a moment. I don't know if I can effect a change alone.

Ghouls are slipping in before me, creeping near.

To the ghouls, as another ghoul, I'm naked, sexless and protoplasmic— cross between bones and wraith-substance.

Why do you want me to talk?

We don't. We're tired of starving; running and migrating. Witnessing massacres and bombings. We don't know if we're tired of being alive or not. You're just another one of us.

I saw a control panel flickering—a minute ago—don't know what it's for.

Its image floats around in Dead, but it's insane. A ghoul says. It was a part of everyone, it's totally nuts.

If I were to catch it, I ask, could I do anything with it?

I don't know, probably. But there's no proof of anything here. What does your proof have broken down?

Did I have a proof? I ask.

Everything you did was like a proof, but the proofs are all broken. Shattered.

And then the keyboard's in front of me again—it's the keyboard this time. I reach out to make notes sound . . .

'Why do you like anything?' That's the song I'm playing, hitting the keys without knowing what I'm doing, enjoying; I don't know the song.

Why do you like anything?
What's any good? Don't know
all my proofs have broken down
all my proofs have broken down

A stupid person, a ghoul says, would say it's good that proofs have broken down. Prove it, you'd say.

I don't know how I can make changes inside this world. This Dead. I'm just another ghoul. Naked, sexless, practically transparent. All of us races look alike, don't we?

Tonight's blood-sacs will be in the shape of shrimps—small, one per victim, bright red. They call us courageous noble people.

No one knows or cares why I'm playing this keyboard. No one knows that my back bursts open while I'm doing it: my back's to the door. My spine feels like it's burning. Burning is good.

If this were the control panel, that would be too easy.

We used to call to something to master us, says a ghoul, but now we run from the butchers.

When they murdered us by remote control, they sang to themselves a lot.

Stop bringing me things, says a ghoul, stop bringing me blood-sacs.

You don't mean that, says another.

I want to migrate again.

Well I want to write something down with the blood in my blood-sac. But it's only enough blood for a short passage. And what will I eat?

Pass on, says another song. Why are you trying? There's supposed to be proof of something. I'm supposed to prove my love, worth, or talent, according to or in reaction to historical precedent: can you hear me calling? I can't stop playing the keyboard. It's effecting no change.

Maybe it is.

Maybe it isn't.

I can't stop playing it.

—

In my remnants self-contained. Because you can't read me. Where I came from or how I became *learned*. (How could it have been *her?*) Someone beyond the Sea taught her; who told me: *nothing*.

The alphabet within grew like flowers, and I was its medium, the *soil*.

In a trial ... patiently ... cutting up ... the masterpiece ... oh that's you. You're cutting me up.

This language in me you can't read, you will *never* decipher. It isn't necessarily historical, my Dark Ray; unless I *am* history. I suppose I am, in Dead.

The other ghouls see through you and your work: *just another job.* We run from you, but we don't think you're very interesting.

It was perhaps a spontaneous language. A record of experience as you said. Or an experiment in beauty, as one finds that statues have been degraded by weather, until their difference from the imagined before is what one cares for.

But maybe it's something else.

So if you had known me as a girl, what would you think of me now? What would *we* think of me now? If this were a silly novel . . . But as one always says, nothing written or made or said corresponds to what's going on. What's going on is a language you can't decipher. Within me I may have an *exact record* of what went on; for, aren't I *magic*? And isn't the language you're finding indecipherable?

But then, you don't really know what I'm up to.

※   ※   ※

Dark Ray has tears, very small ones, in the inner corners of his eyes. Who can he kill? Can he kill this corpse right now?

He says into the mike,"This corpse won't shut up."

※   ※   ※

I don't have a so-called *brain* because I stopped needing one. Or a spine. Though as for the spine-connected-to-hands thing—that operative, musical effect, of course, I can still do that. Make something new come up front from the back or out of the air or ground. There are many *effects* and physiological patterns throughout the body, which itself one might call the brain. But I don't have that any more do I, though *I exist.*

The Greeks were wrong about so much: about gods, war, women, and so on. *Statues.* They thought they had discovered the *body.* I'm sure it's nice to discover something, and Illusion allows all manner of Discovery. Though no one has ever discovered *anything* that improved the lot of women.

So you don't know how you can *hear* me since you can't find something decipherable to *read*? Where do you hear me, in your *ears*? In your head? In the air? Perhaps you're in the process of *discovering* something: what can it be? Would you dare tell anybody? Are you hallucinating?

*   *   *

A question of Dark Ray's self-esteem—something as simple as that. Or some other stamp of a word? YOU ARE A BITCH.

Why does it matter to him? Why does he have to win? Could it be that he'll have a breakdown? Then he could diagnose himself (he's a doctor, after all) and take the pills.

The victim ghouls don't take those drugs. They stare at you and wait for *real food*. Blood-sacs.

*   *   *

When the Greeks discovered the body, they lost timelessness, as real as *I* am.

Now am I supposed to list everything I've seen *down through time* as if that's what timelessness were?

Okay I saw Jason. Jason thought he was happy. He was hilarious, wasn't he?

What is a thought? You think it's neuronal activity corresponding to an interaction between one and one's environment. Wrong. A thought is a cultural imposition, a thing stuck in there by jerks. So Jason thinks, I should be king and that's *all* he thinks—who cares what neurons are up to when there is this *thought* in the world about kings? Which hasn't gone away. You want to be a king, Dark Ray. Girls want to be little princesses, like I once was.

When I rejected *Princess of Colchis*, did I reject my brain, is a good subtle question. I'd say yes. No one could put things in it any more.

The ghouls amassing here call no one's names, Dark Ray. They don't call your name or mine.

Medea ran with her children, as far away from Corinth as she could. It doesn't matter where they went. Was it Media? No this was earlier. Do you remember the old culture? No one remembers it, or do they?

She had directed me to find and open a small box she kept in her room, on the other side of the doorway where I'd stood recently, among the ghouls. Where I'd played the keyboard with pleasure.

The box is plain and wooden, a small coffer. It contains leather surfaces with writing on them (which I don't recognize); several dried flowers in a jar; and a peculiar item which is a cross between a garment and jewelry. It is made of amber beads, fastened together by thread and wire, and would cover the upper torso and hair. The headpiece, wired to the bodice, is a sort of radial tiara, with extensions that create a sunburst effect. The whole item is rather small.

It doesn't fit you any longer, does it.

It's something I can't give up, though I've outgrown it.

Medea ran with her children; they ran and ran. She took the box with her. It explained who she was to herself. As long as she had it, she could explain to her children who they were. It's because this has always been done. A cat or a bird does it differently. Humans teach their children what they've invented.

Medea knew she didn't have to teach them anything, but if she didn't they would be unhappy. They are somewhere in Dead in possession of the language on the skins, the symbolism of the dried flowers invoking magic, and . . . the amber garment?

Why do you outgrow radiance?

I wanted to wear it but I couldn't. Only a child could wear the culture. I kept it as simple as possible for them, since they would insist on "wearing something."

Were you hated for this?

People hate you for whatever you give up.

It must have been so long ago; now we're ghouls, starved for blood, and I can't read the language on the skins.

Sit and listen.

*   *   *

They can't decipher it, because they want it to say what they think. Think they know. In what manner they think they think.

This was the first of the inscriptions left by ghouls, Medea says, that I'm about to recite to you:

Came to kill us in the name of peace and right rule
I knew as a woman I had a pretended say
Especially if I pretended to be generous, radiant, and wise
And they pretended that those were respected qualities.
They now included the conquerors and the male
Conquered. Can I leave you? Can I ever get out of
This world you keep stealing from me?
                                        You
Are an egotist, aetheist, woman without a culture, if you
Take off your garment of light.
                                But I am fleeing with
My culture, I *am* my arts.
                        You have blood on your
Hands.
            I am only eating to go on. Blood of food. I'm
Running now, running with my children.

Migrating across and out of history. They will never let us out; here, children, then, these are the remnants of *our* culture. Hide them from history, hide them from conquerors; show them to no one for no one can be trusted. Our culture will always be a secret among us.

The conquerors are always arriving. The conquerors arrive, I escape. Someone implants their story in my mind, I rip it out, I escape with my children.

There is no radiance, there is no god, nothing you ever said. This is what our writings say. The writings are all tales of Medea, at the end of each of which is written *Medea ran with her children*.

She ran from culture to culture, from mass killing to mass killing.

She helped create Dead so we could live, the writings say.

You will never get her.

There is no way out, you are killing us
or forcing us to become other. I
will always return but who will I be—
a ghoul? Casino: no value: that's that
word. That's where it went. Wandered all
across those continents, looking for a way
off this globe. Go back to the old
Motel, and die like an outcast—"just" a
spirit. You butchers. Leaving nothing but
blood as an allowance in your clement night
you will give us the coin of democracy
so special, invite the survivors to apply for
papers, a progressive and literate dinner. I
don't know where I'm going or who my love is.

When my poems were burned in some lost or future century. Yet I'm
becoming Medea, she's giving me her remnants; needs to go now—die as
they say—she wants that. I will embody her now, take in the stories on the
skins. She's telling them to me before she leaves—at her own will, since she
has no more parts or organs. I will become the one Dark Ray fears and
cannot kill, or dispatch the Club Member to kill. It will simply be evident
that I am the new Medea. Perhaps I will just say it. It's purely psychological
but it's power. Aren't you with me?

Dido will continue to try to found. I will assist sometimes, sometimes
back off to be more purely power, player of keyboard, crackling electric. All
that that *means*. Do I care if anything gets founded? I'm right here, in silly
Dead, alive. And as much in control as anything is. Including the berserk
control panel.

✳   ✳   ✳

Dark Ray into tape: The corpse seems distracted. I get the feeling it's
elsewhere. I've never seen a distracted corpse before. . . Now, I'm beginning
to hear her voice again.

✳   ✳   ✳

So did I represent a so-called people or a so-called sex, at that time? The worst was to be a woman in the thousands of years of prohibitions across culture and class, empire and nation-state (don't you love those phrases? how they roll across a man's tongue.)

But then if they came in to slaughter all of us, all that mattered was the finality of that moment. Because your loves were gone; because you always had some. I'm just sick of it.

(Dark Ray: I'm not sure she's just talking to me.)

There are ciphers for everything I know, but they're almost unnecessary, because you are now like me. Think of them as amber beads, hard light but worn inside. The damned thing's internalized.

I represent the other side of the Cauldron, don't I? But I am a principle of defiance, right? Survival, but not adaptation and change. Don't give in.

It's not that I'm tired, as I may have said. It really is that I'm now empty. Too empty to be part. Empty enough so you can have ... *me*.

✳   ✳   ✳

Dido is lurking, listening: what she does.

Thinks: In order to found my city of ghouls, I may have to get rid of the Club ... Since it is constantly replenished with Members, how can I do this? Something involving the berserk control panel? I've got to put a stop to that Coroner.

This is her ghoul destiny. Found the city, pursue the Club, destroy it. Eat blood-sacs with victim ghouls: how else do you found anything?

And Maat, ah Maat. She's still up there but trembling with weariness. What will happen? What happens when Judgment finally collapses?

✳   ✳   ✳

When my poems were or will be lost. It was because—will be because?— something came for us, a bomb, or vengeful warriors. I remember it as the destruction of all my time until that point. I was a people, shattered. I still carried much inscription inside me.

What more would I tell anyone of myself? I live in a motel that I am fond of. The seediness of my position in Dead satisfies me: so much unchanged.

The ghoul-victims continue to gather in the city.

TESTAMENT:
2005

A RARE CARD

The skills you lack
are designed to keep you
down ...
                    Logical.

Someone is working right now
to get ahead
of you.

Someone is working right now
to get ahead of me.

I have returned
I am reasonably
endowed with the skills of my trade

Those are no longer skills.

———————————

If some power came to me

if some
                    and not meager.
Then

Don't hide. I won't. This
        is provocation

        that's how I'll find it.

Maybe I just do   .
        this

She swallowed the paper she needed;
It contained the
Idea. She must have internalized it.

Words are
drawn to one and soon take over.

No, really, where do they come from?

———————————

Mother of flies
face of the beautiful
corpse

I have
to start.

*Write with a zigzag pencil
and sand.*

———————————

I'm inside the medicine all
the time. This is my
medicine.

Let the words come to the space

who do you talk to if no one reads
it doesn't matter

When someone comes
I'm always there.

Because I drew this very rare
Tarot card, the Witch.

Out in the world they have stories
that match the machine. The one
they appear to be in

If you have walked outside the machine
       who are you?

———————————————

I will enter *their* space
later today & become enraged.
I will know exactly
how much it has cost me
to be a woman.

Here, in magic, it's other

any word
to bring
retrieval.

Mother of flies,
mother of ghouls, of survivors

Form has to be earned. this body

Some voices
will probably talk
       to me

PERHAPS NOT FOR YOU

There is
no
audience
because
there is
no audience.

So if you speak only to
imagined beings
what does "only" mean?

———————————

This building formerly a restaurant . . .
this small room has been scraped of its paint
and denuded of most former furniture: but
also it has grown in size—can a building be
enticed to grow? Because it is now as big as an
airplane hangar.

———————————

Your
      beautiful face
unbloodied beneath
      flies

Mother of flies your
      beauty
to turn to. If only
the audience

could see how
you are peaceful and the
            flies
languid, glossy

But the audience will still bring
            its own feelings
to these
words

not seeing you
            not seeing
what I
am present for.

Who has left me
here, I have.

Who are your
familiars

            Come
      into the
enlarging
page if you dare

      Because he invented
your shape I do mean
structure

because he invented you badly

everything is still hidden.

———————————

I was to impale myself on a
quadrangular
steel rod, with a blunt end
                with a blunt end
which would make puncture
    more difficult
and I tried—it's too hard. I can't
Okay said the voice. I can't
Okay

then I was weeping
                But it's blood! I'm
crying blood! I
screamed

That's part of it
said the voice.

———————————

I think this is hard.
(That's part of it)

How they prefer him must go.

I think this is difficult singing

Length and repetition
    create power

If this voice can return like
    a body

It resembles something that's already been,

Changing.

_____

Chestnuts broken
autumnal fungi
so you will remember. that
        it's fall
outside
        falling. you'll go down

this is no story for the puling
        social classes
No not at all
it's for us my familiars say
who let me weep blood on their ground.

LOGIC

It was a poem
men took because it said *ovary*

didn't take my
political poems
they took the one that said *ovary*

Are you sure it was because it
said *ovary*?

Yes, for them that's *logical.*

———————————

Destroy another
            city
What
else
is war for? So

you'll go down
each of you does. dies in
                        whirlwind

each of you who does, dies
            paying
for the pain you experience
            Just that
and nothing is established

Because I am a woman

Cutting as many cords
as tie you to me. this isn't
        anarchy
it isn't anything you
        could name

You're still here
without ties?

because they were *logical*.

———————————

Dance little asshole dance
oh he gets elected, like a Calvinist
He says, I have these guts
Men, I have these guts.

———————————

Having dedicated whole
regions to the destruction
        you inspire, the
logic will be to go on doing it
doing it. Having proceeded by

the logic
        of your per-
sonal vaccuum
you will perceive your continued
        lightlessness
as an excuse to go on. having
gone on
as you have. And so one continues.

_____

Lead the boy out of
        the building on fire
his head twisted
        upwards
all fucked

What else is there to
        know if
one has gotten
twisted up
all fucked

he is a screaming fire

_____

In the explanations
of our lives' experience

they've left out this wild moment
the long mirror on the right-hand wall of the
corridor suddenly shattered
I can't see myself anymore.

_____

I repeat that I am not frightened
        and why not
I don't know
what my reactions
are supposed to be.

―――――――――――

"Please tell me something
with which I 'm familiar."

isn't there another part of now

WITHIN THE NO-CHANGE
COIN PURSE

She has no defense for
what's happening
Cannot defend

herself against them, even
when they want to
defend her.

In my own arms
I have no recourse.
Inside myself will I die

because you want to
save my country
who am I?

––––––––––––––––

I will meet you in the autumn
        of my
life—what will I wear?
A big black hat with roses or
some lace—
        why?

God told you to.

God told me to tell you.

God always knows what
you should wear.

––––––––––––––––

'It is not that women must
obey me, I am enlightened.
It's that I don't really want to
          think
about them or what they say,
and I don't have to.'

———————————

I saw my sister in a store
carrying a small notebook
she had decided to write her own
          praises
no one else would

we were selecting tiny
          things, pretty vials
for our pleasure/necessity/
          unknown. I even
stole some. There was a
          justification

of this petty theft
I only need petty things, after
          all.

I
     shouldn't need anything
as large as power.

———————————

          Ready

her again

READY?

this space, in this space. one
destroys. with these petty
stolen vials, I will destroy
        god

In this ritual,
respect for all religion
is banished.

GO.

(leaves.)

_____

What does the Witch card look like?

She wears a blue down coat
because she is rather
        deep.

_____

So, I—I say—and in the
parking lot near the first
self or person, the self-named
father of Reason, a cop, drove
his motorcycle in threatening
circles around her.

She stood perfectly still
in her blue coat.

pieces of dusty logic. why
say
        that I don't have to remember
anymore what they are
what it is.

        I don't believe in the universe
any
more.

ANOTHER PART OF NOW

I find you where the
     body is. You are the body.
This body is everything.
     But isn't me. Is it me?
I didn't kill it but have
     to dump it. I'm on the dumping-
     off train.
Which stops at "Judas" and
     "Through": same thing. I'll
     leave you off.
You could just be America.
     Why would anybody keep
     America?
All the poor dumb fucks
     have nothing else to keep. You
     poor dumb fucks,
If my name is Judas
     I'm not hanging myself from
     a beautiful redbud tree.
Do you know what I've
     been through? Was it ever
     worse for you?
Or I could say, This corpse is
     the one you killed. And you'd
     gape at me.
If I say it to myself, what's
     that? that I killed it?
Maybe I killed the whole
     thing. I had a gun once
I've had razors, poison, and
     knives.
I was always afraid I would kill. Americans
     can't get by
     without weapons.

And so, there's a body. Did I
        bend over you to
        help you?
But what if I violated you—vulnerable
        you—
        because I could?
I have to go, someone
        says. Have to go fight for
        America.
But there's nowhere else,
        he says
        There's nowhere else but here
Go to another country,
        still feels like our flesh. And
        kill some one.
Okay I will. I can do that.
        Now the body bag's on
        this train.
I've got to get rid of it
        at Judas. Then
        I'll be Through.
Who's ever through? Even
        if you're dead you're not
        through.
I know because the dead
        talk to me. It's
        never over, they say.

I'm afraid you're the body. But
        I'm not really afraid. I don't
Know what I'm supposed to be
        afraid of now.
If you're an
        American—if you're the
        body—
I'm not saying you died of fear.

Scared they were going to
kill you.
Some of them were inside your
system. Viruses and serial
killers
Terrorists breaking through the
fragile borders of this chaos
held to-
Gether by fear of being. I've had
that too. But if I've lost you,
I'm lost. Losing it, finally old
enough. You don't
have a word in your throat,
Says a haunter voice. Not a
pretty word. But I'm carrying
the body of my
Country. Or my own. My lovely
body. Or *him*, again?
What a strange word
That pronoun is. When I call
myself *she* I just laugh.
I want you to know
That I care about you; though
I've said I don't care
about anything now.
I see the pasty face of a white
woman. But
I see everyone else
Somber inside me; I'm
not sure I see the rich.
Can I
Include them in the caring? I
want *you* to know where
my heart is.
But I don't *know*, like I don't know
if you're dead.
The corpse doesn't have to be

You. 'I've made it,' you say,
        'I'm not dead.' Who has
        the power here?
Not *her*, this blood blossom
        woman. We've created a
        dead girl?
There was a mistake I made
        about who would take care
        of her. It turned out not
To be you. You told me she was
        already free, had the vote.
        What a jerk
You were. She's still defunct;
        who has the power,
        really?
I know I don't, I'm
        just talking. Voice in
        Singer.

I have to sing my way
        out of here. I'm crowded
        with old corpse
Furniture. Inside me is my
        country I take
        everywhere. Though
You don't know me, I talk to you.
        I'm supposed to be like
        all of you; but what am *I*
Like? That's what I can't
        remember. These times are
        for the select
Diagrams of status blown off a
        dead tree. It's not 'our
        group'; it's all
The star group. Doesn't
        relate to you. Except
        as you're used

Can't I find new words?
        But I saved all these
        words for
You. I can't see what you ever
        knew, all that dust in the
        middle of our map. I
Killed it, you killed it, Mother of
        Flies, a beauty. She looks
        peaceful. It would be
Good to remember what
        someone's supposed
To do. Before all you
        are the body. I haven't been
        able
To speak without a corpse near-
        by for thirty years. What
        does birth ask of us,
My people? That's all we
        want to know. So talk to
        the question, can't it
Answer you, tell you
        before you are stolen
        away?
The whole world
        supposes you
        powerful
But power hasn't occurred
        to you. Her mouth was
        always crooked from
Uncertainty. She talked like
        me but had a nicer
        voice. I'm not here to
Make everyone else
        happy or
        uncomfortable. All
Our cabals dissolve in dis-

traction, then take up
   again when you get lonely.
What's a cabal? you say, I
   never get all of what
   you're saying.

Do I have to get rid of Judas?
   I'm afraid you won't have
   come this far with me,
Because you don't read.
   That's fair enough; I'm
   asking for special attention. But
This is the story of your dead
   body, lying under
   accusation of misuse of
Power. Power. Don't you
   want its secrets? You
   sweetly say no. Don't you
Know you *were* it? Someone
   used all your
   substance:
We're what they had. The
   gift to our leaders. We
   wouldn't
Know how to conquer any-
   thing. Not even for
   God. As for country,
That's us. I am your Judas,
   because I'm telling. What you
   can't stand: Truth.
It always hurts you and you
   cry. You escape again and
   they win of
Course, make your children
   soldiers, reduce your income,
   calling that freedom

'I have so much freedom I
        can give it away. It's like
        air here.'
Okay, that's your poem. And you
        don't want the gold
        ornamenting the skull,
under flies. Someone
        already grabbed it
        anyway;
She came to us stripped, this
        body. Who could be your Foreign
        Victim. But
You only care about your
    ·   own,
        it's always how they
Mistreated one . . .
        I can't get rid of it
Can't dump the body.
        Decays in time. There's
Never been any time here.
        I got this old without
        feeling it. And
See, I still talk like you. I
        must be the Mother
        of Flies,
Not Judas. Get back up and
        walk right out of
        here. They can
Use you some more, you
        know
        even if your substance is
Rotten. Live and be part of
        their power. See if they
        care.

VOICE IN SINGER

Writing her own praises,
she must be life. the wind

"Maybe
Identification of

Voice
in Singer

This willful
Identification

causes
agitation."

Said the voice apart from me.

Nothing here—is it?—but
this voice.

Voice: Audience

Voice: And dialogue itself was
        almost gone.

Now I'm in a blanket green whose
white designs mean . . . that I'm
wearing

a vocal
source. So each word see the

ones on shoulders, spirals,
are probably glyphs for
        'Emergence.'

The people walked up my throat and
emerged from my mouth . . .

it was the only thing I was
for.
Why?
Because *for*
because *for*
has no meaning. Unreluctantly

    I have nothing
        to vaunt at this time ex-
cept for my
blanket
which doesn't exist

The syllables are so warm.

————————————————

'You can never see where you've come from.'

Judas rubies burned in her
ear, for all she could hear
the voice produced on this site

no presentiments, if you are
there. can't know the
next,

as you expect a sense of familiar-
ity, but these
are
unexpected
familiars.

———————

There is a free woman there
with her arms up high
in a dance.

I saw her without having to.

I can't find compulsion anywhere.
in this place, now

———————

No monitors.
The man bent over flute an
        old locust.

I know what I'm doing
the only I knowing
in this voice
Are you a figure
Do you have a you
Have
it isn't a matter of possession

———————

Without compulsion

the thoughts that come
        would be useless to
resent

this present
at last
what
can last?
It
can.

BENEATH THE SLAB

Where the Slab was, walking
across the terrible water, I
concluded the crossing. I lifted the grey
Slab and walked through
      the watery
mass, its dirt, and bugs, and also
red and blue morning glories.

—————————————

Can you upgrade my ticket
     she asked?

—————————————

You might upgrade your ticket,
if you know some stories of
middle-management people
who safely land an airplane

when the pilot has been in-
capacitated. I know one, she says,
involving a woman. Tells anecdote
remembered from Reader's Digest.

Do I get the upgrade?
The man says, you *may* get an upgrade
after you tell the story again
when you present your ticket at the

counter. Can I still use my old ticket if
they won't accept my anecdote? No, he says.

———————

What is a witch? cut word
it is a myth but
may have to use. if
I've lost my original ticket.
    this land
only accepts one myth of
    origin

but what *I* call witch
will be different

Because I can call it.

So I'm just calling it with
some of my materials.

———————

Just another dead guy
frying a hamburger.
"They'll screw your ass
right into the ground," he
said. He said it twice,

"They'll screw your ass
right into the ground."

———————

Frontally, I might be
    invisible.

I don't have a valid but
know this is safe, because

it's
        a dark green
morning.

—————————

I thought the machines contained
holy men, flying off the ground

priests taking off but this
isn't levitation, it's machines.

One who survived a crash
                        They're
pulling her out of the plane.

"He's okay," said the man next to me,
though the test pilot who survived
        the crash
was a naked woman.

—————————

I still couldn't see the point of
anything. surviving for love
of myself—

the pain can be overwhelming.

Do you want to look at it?

No, I want power

You don't want me to ex-
    press myself.

Not here, No. That's exactly
what I don't want.
You muddled my ticket
why should I even
need a ticket?

GLORY

The name   of   Gloria   is
  morning glory
you could walk right into it
and
greet I forgot.

     no
reason

You are my word

The name of power forgotten is
morning glory.

   —————————

I was starved
and they had nothing
except for Gloria's
name, their relation

this is pathetic bread
bought on Broadway

Walk out and get food,
mother said.

Sorrow comes as a consequence

treat it as a malleable
substance, blue or green
red red for glory. no blue

green. I am green
holding up blue or red

Because of the beautiful
medieval
conceit, the flower and the leaf.

———————

White woman, leave me alone.

———————

It's flowing through me
for no reason
all this power—for no reason,
        for reason

When you enter the food
        chain as form,
what do you eat?

The body strewn globe bids
        you welcome

But I've been *here* before.

———————

Do you remember when you
first realized people
were willing to kill each
other for almost no reason?

———————————

seeped into the blood, or
water supply

something I said. or did.

———————————

What do you have to
        say
You're cruel
I'm not
I'm not the one like that.
But everyone
says that
You didn't *have* to make
        it into a club

you didn't have to
what did you have to
do? I was starved and wanted
        some bread
you had a club for killing people
I didn't have it / Someone has it
Kill them you said
I didn't say that
Someone said it. Who said it?
I know a guy who said it
        you're so naive
If you have to kill people because you're
        born
why not have a club for it
if you

there is no one here. There's
no you here!

———————————————

Your leg is shaking you've been to war
Is that a reason?

You called me White Shell Woman
so I would be here.

I won't let you die I went
        back for you, though
I'm just a word

There's a night where you
        don't say words
Do you know that?
No I don't know it

LA DISCONNECTING

It was a fat hairless man wearing
a t-shirt with an image of
Jean hyphen Something Something
the icon in charge of the process
called *La Disconnecting*.

_____

What happens if
about sincerity, I
am *sincere*, no Sorry
I don't want that.

_____

That world is not here. even if it
kills me

_____

Where the mirror broke
She went down there many
times,

She is asking a man to aid her
but they are not pronouns.
They both have grey hair. He puts
things in her hands sometimes. Stones.
Nothing you would value. What
these figments, of which I am one, value.

———————————

Having become almost old
I feel gratified to have
aged but don't know why. The

guy pressed a two-dollar
bill to the lapdancer's bad
knee, is the inversion
of this genre.

———————————

It was on my way down
here that the mirror
shattered.

Sometimes I see face in
fragment—a
past me?

Of the t-shirt image of
Jean hyphen Something Something:
Can I change it to me if
I don't know what I look like I
don't want him in charge of
La Disconnecting.

———————————

I'm not being methodical
         having been
shattered. I can't find
      the

where you ask it
where you're supposed to
        believe *it*

———————————

I'm down here
the figment people
comfort me, over
and over. I seem to need so

much comfort
Because you just play
at it. (who) and the sound
of us nothing

———————————

As the morning darkens

gradually change it

in La Disconnecting
what are you making

the Sound.
                It will tell you
how to be
it always does

———————————

A city destroyed but
populous

returns for my
political soul.

a light keeps that's
mine hands lips and hair

I am the way forward

in La Disconnecting.

AFTER LIGEIA

Show myself dead ... you're squinting
Do I have to cover my head
    like some
damned cultural scrap
Look at my bone, you're
    shaking ... !
Break it up, the cops
You'll never stop me now,
    not this ghoul

isn't. Ice flower trees out your
    window, dark
I wasn't broadcast all over the
    place.
Who made me? if I was/am
    always
the subjective factor

perceived but whose power was
    mute
now

I've come to predict your
    death: Oh
can't you *handle*
    a ghost? you
can *handle*
everything else, so you say.

Name me. just try to

everyone some damned scrap
    on their

heads to show that they
        cower
are pure. And those who
        don't
arrogant as proof. Let's
        get past that I'm
dead. I have the haunt's
        power
and you can't subdue
        me.
Come to you out of some tale
in one of your horror
        periods, to
slowly twist your neck. You
        can't stop it:

those are the rules.

                Soldiers came
to maim and foresake you sent
        them—you
stayed at home, thinking. Oh wasn't
        that useful?
Didn't want to kill, perhaps
But aren't I dead? We
were equally anonymous: your
        anonymity
has slain me: my plan is to
        scare you to death now.

First, a short, true
        history
which means *unfair* parti-
        culars
I don't refer to what you do,
        or even to what
my so-called people

think should be referred to.
　　　My history
is subjective, get it?
　　　There was a
child went forth (I can
　　　translate you—
can you do me?)
Oh yes child, he and then
　　　she:
they hesitate there
　　　and leave her
precious musings to herself,
　　　so considerate-
ly—and the *she's* can have their
　　　own
power structure. *Because*
they like that!
　　　God con-
structed our differences
　　　Or,
some other abstract convenience
　　　did, maybe an
ethereal stove or
washing machine! Go
　　　where you're fated.

I didn't just go where I was
　　　supposed to
I had a *second* body, which
　　　functioned all on its
own, thinking—as you would
　　　call it—
its *un*surfacing excursions
that body being who I am
　　　now.
So one *un*blustering child
　　　went forth

a little girl. And didn't they
        love her for
herself? So *un?*

But you're
        shitting scared
of her.
O, I see, the wraith of teeth,
        skull, hair—
classic. Just so you'll recognize
        me.
Who was I beautiful, young?
        Well I *wasn't*
I was what *I* say. If you look
through your own
        beautiful
glue-sockets, bulbous glops
        of nerves—
who knows what you'll see?
I looked from my
cynical covered head at masses
        of clumpy up-
rights by the flowing
        liquid burning
orange-silver. Those were some
        scraggy trees, and
two-legged you's,
        moral pea-brains. Yes I
remember my girlhood

It's heat near the Euphrates, or
        wherever
We live in an ancient city
We are practically ancient aren't we
        we wear
kohl and have *customs:* you
        don't have

customs, because you're always
          our judges
Jealous judges relinquish nothing
          to their
petitioners. Sack that city
          of forgeries!
You recognize my language?
          it's
poetry, my other body
          You're scared
of a song, you coward . . .
I'm telling you a story, from
          between the same nude
teeth I always had.
          You're
so glad you can be here,
          where
the war doesn't go. No?
          You're
privately sad? Sad privates
smoke behind screens
          somewhere else.

I entered a room in my
          youth, where
obviously I
          was blessed. And
there was a lot of warm
          bread; and
so much affection. They
          treat you gently
our ways are so
          rich. Do they prepare me
for death after
          a life-time
of being secondary? But
          we're treated

honorably; proud of our
lineage; probably generous
        gash by your
standards. Do
I tell it how you've
        heard it?
Isn't this *interesting*? Our
        gender skills
Do something skillful. I
        didn't want to
do anything,
        except think. Familiar?

Do I meditate on power or
        on hatred? I'm
still here, so you can feel the
        force of
this . . . *unnameable*. I'm here
        to help you
lose breath.
Everyone was choosing
        Or
there were no choices; had
        been made,
there were cheeses, traditional
        passages, massages
the tedium so weighty. I found
my other body—composed of a
        poem-like
substance,
how, what? You'd have to spend
        a lifetime
doing it
out of *need*, not vanity. So
        this other body

This other body went forth with
        its night-
mare prayer: that it have all
        the power it
needed, to be as important as
        I felt. In my
singularity: sanguine sanity; for
        the only sense
I could find was in myself. I
        am the world
always inventing it.
        And
I'm dead, what does that
tell you—that anyone may be
        making it up
As I do stand here before you.
        How can that be?

So can you handle what's
        really
unfamiliar—me? un to the
        senses *you* exploit: *yes*
you were given all to
        know. If you
have it, don't you know it?
        And if you
know it, how can you help that?
        Sure, I was
had: women are. Price-seeking
        persons keep us from
having as much
        as them. Men
don't want to compete with
        women.
I'd be content to be un-
        speaking dead if

you'd have let me *in*! Until you
    do
I can only work
    to kill you back.
We're almost equal in combat
I'm subjective, but you're a
    hoax.
Completely made up
    body of
your competences:
your face is plastic.
You can see how it wavers
    Your head that
squishy mass—no second
body for you—
    A head's

squishier if it's blasted open.
Don't you just want
    to clean that up? Scrub
our brains off the floor? So
    your daughter
can maneuver her dress
    through to her
perfect school.
I was trying I was trailing
    No, you weren't
there, gentle aren't you?
After I hear my own *screaming*:
    I'm in a time
compromised, I
meant to say
    comprised, oh I
meant! But time got
    hypnotized
at the mercy of a power
    which I am granted

by myself, by the entity
    below
the dreamer: *this* body escaped
    time like any poem

Are we breathing? I'm
    not.

They photograph us primitive
    women
weeping, shouting, waving
    signs—must want to be
seen in that frozen
era. You've three times killed her,
one for the photo
    one
for the body and one for the
    boding your
ethics love, that fear of me
    catching up to
you
    and look!
Here I am! an official dead
    civilian!
Take an anti-depressant! I'm not
    supposed to
know that. You
    can say *ziggurat*—
can you say splat, clot, shit,
    horizontal?
No leverage for drainage, can't get the
    blood down
the pipe.
    So, no,

I'm not interested in
    your soul.

Or those of the factional farts
     everywhere
worshipping something: like you
worshipping what
you know.
How wrong it all is. But I'm
     not. You a
soul who didn't
couldn't, the mark of your own
     confidence
game. Protoplasm,
     you are
no one
except he who horrified
     sees me.

My song kills yours.

I always knew I'd be left standing.

THE WORLD I'M DEAD IN

I don't remember what happened
    in order,
Because there was no order
But the events had weight, and
    feeling.
The World I'm Dead In.

————————————

Where am I unfounded mercury
    too rapid the assessing of
One. (lifetime.) He doesn't know where
    it is. (world.) The scientific
command given over, too; I
    let them have it all.
I need to find you and tell you but

I can't remember the order of
    events
Because "order" is different here.

————————————

The intermezzo swells
    that I used to
know.

Do you like this death?

It's a European kind of
world but the order—two
        women are
studying oranges, the
        color
while Brahms swells because
        it's after the end of
my century—in order, I'm
        not dead, really.

The tidal wave's part of this milieu
that you've always dreamed of
        crashing over
the desert, millions of years

Where are you going,
to the California Palace of the
        Legion of Honor?

——————————

Frankly you don't need
        consecutive order.

I sat starkly in the waiting room
waiting to be told I was dead;

Was this by executive order

Death was a blonde and wore a
black leather jumpsuit.
Her dog wore a black leather
dog jacket.

I had to pat the dog
As in *From Now On.*
In the hospital, near a
bland window.

—————————————

Since the shattering of the mirror
along a way down, I've
        thought of

identity as over. Yet this
        Voice
reappears
as a force against
seduction into
the death voice of my
supposed
times.

—————————————

The wind through no trees
        there are none
in this *quartier.*
Singled you out deliberately for
        a hatred
that was, it was said, in the racial
memory. What one might
        want to
Destroy. Die out of. the racial
        memory.
You woman.

Meet you again, at Le Corail
meet you inside

Dead world I am so alive in or
    vice versa.

THE ARROW LUSTER

      Pushing on
through
endless layers
of words—

'to be my own master I warned you.'

––––––––––––––––––

This famous orchestra
conductor proposes
a vague intermixture
of the feminine
in his masculine

        Because there's no woman
in the room? What is he
    talking about?

    There is no
    feminine/masculine.
    There is what
    I say.

––––––––––––––––––

Even insults
create grief:
          it's not enough
to silence you
    by killing
your close ones in war

(with grief you won't care
        any more. Would this be
'feminine' of you?)

_____

Voice: Women are simply the best that
        we have.
If you die soon, you may not have
        gotten
everything you might have wished for
That could happen to anyone
It's chancy to be a poet. We only
        insulted you when
you misbehaved or weren't up to our
        standard . . .

_____

Do you remember when you were
        asked
to stop reading your poetry onstage
        three years ago—
You had supposedly exceeded the host's
        time limit—
The genius who'd earlier read a poem
comparing his phallus
        to an artichoke?

_____

Do you remember the famous poet, drunk
(you'd written just a few poems then)
who, in front of a roomful of people, asked if

you were wearing "any underwear at all?"
Fell red-faced down on the floor
beside his wife's feet.
                    Killed himself some
        years later.

——————————————

After I'd written "White Phosphorus,"
        an elegy
for my brother the veteran,
a man presumed to tell me
what white phosphorus was

as if I hadn't written the poem.
This man hadn't been near the
        Vietnam War.

——————————————

EMOTION AS STRUCTURE

        Delete most of the list
        of insults accumulated
        during lifetime as poet.
        All-
        right;

They'll just call you a
        complainer

And nothing matters now.

——————————————

Emotion, defined as an outburst
and not the structure of
    his acquisitiveness,
    has led to a logic of
             domination.

It is not emotional to flash
    one's artichoke
It is emotional (not factual) to write
    an elegy.

———————————

I went down there and saw the figments
again. *The most beautiful thing I can
do.* Has no relation to
    sympathy for you.
      A beauty reason falls into
place with, glowing
      the sounds between the vocal sparklets . . .

The ingenuity that could have been its own
reward he wanted
to kill you off
with, buy you off—what's the difference?

    He has lost it; it's mine.

THE COLOR OF ALTARS

Someone's dying, an unjust failure
"Didn't do right" says a stick.

Night after night I'm asleep.

Another one leaves when I wake up
He's dead, right? Yeah—kind of nuts

changed all the brown figurines.
They have labels; can't read them

It was my *generation*
this home was my church, am I
        going away

Everything's so brown
The color of altars.

———————————

    Trying to remember the happiness
of numbers, I *was*. If you were a cipher,
without identity, filled with bliss a worker
among workers: could understand that?
A reddish rounded metal shape, the face, it
was so modern. The ones who railed
against identity always had a position—
more than opinion; a professorship, even a
chair: was the furniture talking? I hated
that, so I had an identity. Felt bad about
hating, then the century changed. He was
still more or less in place; and I was just crazy,

in society, what was that? A gun, pointed at
its own head.

———————————

Trying to remember, I was.
You're not supposed to say it, so I-ishly
Who else has been around for ages?
A new pronoun: *shithead* . . .
It has taken me 59 years to achieve
this quality of perfect desertion.

———————————

The silliness of the Kingdom.
Go, stay, whatever. I'm
the possessor of the language;
what difference does it make
where I live?

. . . mad at me because she
thinks I'm belittling
my (our) country; as if I might
value her opinion: I'm allowing
her to represent everything I
can't have time for, like countries.

———————————

Now it's amber-colored insects
dense in a layer stretched all

along the ceiling of a hallway.
I follow this overhead pathway

to a room where a woman
had fit together insect pieces

constructing a voice to trap me,
lure me into the amber stratum;

into a death, and it almost worked
we almost managed to kill you,

she says, but we didn't have
enough stuff.

———————————

It has taken me 59 years to achieve
this quality of perfect desertion

I didn't leave you; didn't even
put on my jacket.

But have no choice but not to die

There are different ways not to die
the one that has chosen me

is not popular.

———————————

As you see
these ancient ceramics of
fishes
gradually become
more transparent but also more
fiery

a handprint of fire or if
blue, iridiscent—why
are you leaving
when I'm explaining in the
style of a poem
how this art
progresses over the
centuries
as if I'm its maker,
always?

I didn't leave, I never leave;
you leave
who can't stay the poem.

———————————

Any word
will not desert me

I know, the figment says.
and everything old brown as in
        the legend

I have achieved by
suddenly coming alive

out of a fish fossil—it was
dangerous, and is, whatever I do

from now on.

EVERYDAY

In the call for you, do you . . .
"I gave you . . ." someone begins.

     Words call
and figures who wish to move

"I gave you . . ."

—————————————

Everything's supposed to be a
          debt—
Doubt
that

—————————————

Preordained because of the
buildings you walk
between.
          Centurions

escort me to the tomb of
I gave you.

          Consent to
be
a mythological figure

          Greek or cinematic
Sure.

Ma, or grand, latinate
my love. I love you (I gave you)

———————————

It has finally become only
language. Where are my
words? An example,
behind the arras at Arras; the
difficult situation is avoided
by having the woman at
the tomb be one of the three
nudes in Cranach's The
Judgment of Paris. She is,
in fact, Dido. who wasn't
one of them. That doesn't matter.

———————————

There was something I had
        never seen before
twisted green
a torsolike life thing
        floating
in a tunnel. Nobody wanted it.

———————————

I think it's beautiful
Might be alive
entered the food chain, night of
        survivors

where I turned and begged, in
        states of soul,
to be released from mere daily life
        again.

                You
could die alive rag people,
        in a
        torn
terrain, no blossoms. Signs
theirs each's meaning fell into
        place
He says it; then you. released
        back to jammed up
speakers. Screaming/stifled

you can find something even more
        fallow/fetid/
fallacious, if you succeed

if your language
        sticks to the formula

that wanders about the city
sweating glue.

———————————

The form I'd never seen before
makes its way towards
me.

Existing it can be
logically
existing

imploring,
I am the real
Dido,

I founded a city

I am still doing that
behind the tapestry
of me
as lovesick
     suicide
Help me find my
voice (city, my voice is
     your
city.)

FROM TESTAMENT OF THE GHOULS

Death was blonde and wore a black leather jumpsuit. Her dog wore a black leather dog jacket; I was commanded to pat the dog.

If you pat the dog, you become a ghoul. You are then playing by different rules from the *living* living; you do not adhere to the city's established narrative sequences. You aren't in that book, you're in this one, where you are unconscious.

Don't you know you're unconscious right now? No?

I patted her dog, who'd come near me as I lay on a hospital bed by some bland window. It's that dog, it's always that dog—I know it means *her*.

Sure I had one of the viruses. So far so normal.

It is a planet of disease. There are many many viruses, affecting the organs selectively. The viruses come from everywhere, and there are more each year. People die, perhaps as many as are killed in the genocides; so there are always more ghouls everywhere.

The ghouls speak in "poetic" language, because they are souls whose stolen lives have been "prolonged" by the *poetic* within them. The only aspect of the human that hadn't been analyzed and "understood." As people lost interest in it, it secretly became them. It is all that lives in one; but what if I am wicked—that is a poem. You are alive and can't die. Do I know I'm alive. You are unconscious while you read this.

Everyone is connected to a war somewhere, possibly to an ongoing genocide. Who sweeps the graves?

Each country has a primary city; maybe two or three; it has a king-twit who oversees the army. If the king-twit is elected, he is the elected commander of the killers he may assemble if he so chooses. So far so normal.

None of the king-twits seems to be aware of the amassing of the ghouls. Our ghoulish souls, poems slipping by the normal death-laced lives of the capital, slipping between you and gathering invisibly near the great *gares* at night and along the dirty river with its pollutant-malformed fish. More cars full of diseased patients, death chariots, the poisonous toys of lesser twits and twitesses; we slip through, we fly past, we gather. We gather and gather.

Such a mean-spirited god. That you had to pray to it. It the little human prayed to it the little god—that was how they deserved each other; so there's always something left to the little human: the little god. And if you won't pray to it, it will implague you.

The ghoul Josepha had been a woman who had no foundation, as privately a cynic she didn't allow the god in. When she succumbed to the pustules she didn't budge in her secret disbelief, though she let everyone pray over her what else could she do. She couldn't move and there they were hovering at bedside.

The whole life had been ridiculous, she thought. She hadn't any idea why she'd had to do it, though being dead had never promised better than being alive. Maybe she really did love clothes and makeup, cars, who knows what I loved? They told me what it was: clothes, makeup, a job, someone else.

She turned her face away from her friends and away from the direction of the Coliseum where the Jesus-Freaks fried up non-believers on an immense grill, but you already know all this stuff, and don't care. You get off on the smell of burning flesh.

And so who do I write to as ghoul of no class with this outcry in my hand and the story where we without stars in our crowns crawl finding blood to lap up?

I've told some of this history before. But the molecules of the perceived world of ghouls are shifting again: and once more, to whom do I speak? Do you love me? Lost so much weight we're invisible crowding the masterpiece foyer of the architecture of our former masters.

The blood-sacs have still to be explained. The fact that our souls are poems is obvious, once it has been stated—in a book or in an oral tradition, the statement of the obvious is possible. In the technological arts one doesn't really say things. Rather the work enters the audience's mind as monolithically as it can so it won't suffer loneliness—either the audience or the artwork.

And so who do I write to, no one. I am the activator of our ghoul world because as I record 'my mind' we see each other, our quaint whiteish forms. I am helping us to wait for what we're owed, after the planet is finished and the gods all of them are defunct, the diseases are exhausted, and the geno-cides, successful, are concluded.

Who will pay us what we're owed? A preoccupying question since there will be no one there, but I think we presume to agitate the air throughout the lengthy degradation all are participating in; ask but no one hears, staring back at our invisibility.

Who provides the blood-sacs we eat? Is it a force generated by ourselves?

Josepha, for example, drinks the blood. What difference—she thinks—does it make what she does? Drinks the Blood and Waits for What's Owed provide as much structure as she's prepared to tolerate. In ancient wherever it was, there was interminable structure, of hours and chores, of debts to the leaders and the gods, of grooming rituals, of supposed pleasureable activi-ties, of meals, sexual congress: one served the interfaces with all one's overflowing what? My image cries out unto you—rush towards, rush towards! Why had no one ever determined Josepha was cynical?

I tell Death the leatherclad that she has no art. How do you figure that my dear, she says clawing my hair, stroking me in the classical manner. You arrive in an instant, doing nothing, making nothing. She smiles at me in failure of intelligence. Your dog is more frightening than you are, I say. Your dog means you, you mean nothing. She continues to stare vacuously.

I Dido stood in cemeteries far behind the arras that depicted me. I didn't kill myself, I stood around by graves. Obstinant the Sidonian to, in my primal aspect, be more amazing than in their virility, the poet and his locutions. What fate follows me, born of no goddess, through so many perils made inconsequential for being a feminine name? How can I speak so twisted in tongue as to have come to be added to *his* name and *his* praise—his language, and I called lover not a founder fortune-driven? Yet who hasn't heard of me?

Dido stands, skeletal, on the dirty marble steps, doorway to the maw of the stock exchange: anyone has devalued us in there; they do so now.

Do you feel the December cold, ghoul? As once, honored, into the divine temple you were led.

You can see her skull and her ribs, you can see the pubic bone beneath the pale veil of ghostliness, for we are equals waiting: how do we distinguish one from another? No one was ever an individual was she? Wasn't I educated that the perceived unique essence is socially inflected, an inculcation?

I transmit to you my fame, from my bone to yours.

The woman with no arms speaks: on your same continent, Dido, I lost what you have—can you see that? How are we able to know us? Is Death an idiot of so little skill in her negative talent, that she can reduce us to equality in ghoulishness but not destroy 'what happened'?

No one can destroy what is happening to me, a soldier speaks, for I still smell gutted flesh. Can you see that I'm tainted?

We see ghoul, but we know who you are. We can know who each is even in the myriad count where we throng, as I am dead, says the speaker, and unconscious see the clarity of your form.

The machine of genocide was in place, she says. Then the murderous furor spread through all of the country. Why, Dido, do you boast of your name, when many of us fell from machete blows or lost all to torture? What else can be real?

I am a name, Dido says, it is my fate to be branded. Don't you have your own? your own lie-name? she asks the woman.

Nothing matters, says the woman, except to wait for my arms.

All ages blending or blinding here. When waiting begins it has always been and then your story has no context save for the ghoulishness of this condition.

Josepha the cynic who died of plague is branded by her maleish name and her lack of explanation.

All the great religions failed, with everyone frantic to practice them. Josepha talks to Christian ghouls, Buddhist ghouls, Muslim ghouls, animist ghouls, sectarian ghouls. Ancient pagan ghouls of every polytheism. They're all puzzled because it didn't happen: whatever their divinities or doctrines predicted didn't arrive. No unearthly afterlife, no reincarnation, no nirvana, no return as soul of tree or stone, no being transmitted into pure racial flow, nothing as simple as atheistic-type extinction. No. We're all ghouls. It's as if we're permanently trapped in some form of blasphemy, an existence that's blasphemic to almost everyone.

Josepha isn't puzzled, having had no expectations. To be a whey-faced fuzzy blood-lapper is as reasonable a fate as any other she had heard of.

I thought I would be somewhere nice in my best younger body, happy, a ghoul says. Josepha laughs.

There's a discarded compact; open it and look at yourself.

In all the history of the ghouls, does the same ghoul visage suffice, does one face the same ghoul regard no matter who opens the compact?

Is this nothing but ghoul, face of my eyes?

Face of my nose and mouth?

This is the species *ghoul* looking back at you: in type you have reproduced, but you do *know* you are you.

If someone calls you across a hundred ghostly bodies, it is because you are ever detectable.

Where do the blood-sacs come from? Scattered to us twice a day by arms even more ghostly than ours? Where does our purpose—propensity to wait—come from?

The future starts to appear, the far side of it first. Death is showing us something.

She doesn't know how.

Where do the rules for cruelty come from?

To practice torture your back sits approving: stiff but rippling, satisfied.

This came from nowhere in nature, says a ghoul: nature is dull.

Are we in nature? says another.

Death is showing us something; she doesn't know how.

She stands near Dido, with an eyebrow arched, though we know she's too stupid for irony. 'I know what irony looks like,' she says.

Death is dumb but beautiful: is she always blonde and blue-eyed? No. But I am seeing her that way, Josepha says.

The woman with no arms sees her as African, smiling in empty malice.
Cemeteries, the little huts they build for us, which we don't inhabit.
Everything we did for Death was as empty as she is.
I am now building the city with my feelings, Dido says.
Do you have them?
Try to find what Death doesn't have. But if she isn't very smart, her
erasures are powerful, for here we are in ownership of nothing but ourselves.

You are Dido, founder of a city draped in the red cloth of the individual.
For when you saw him leave progressively smaller in the harbor, your
vulnerable wound fed the very foundation of this civil pact, that the mirror
show us equals, citizens.
Because he left, am I not worthy of you?
I remember a sumptuous cloth: what if it were all that I needed?
I need my own arms cries that other. Retribution for the ghouls is not a
light topic, citizens, she says. In this civil gathering of cheated souls, we will
create a psyche of the deserted which contrives to render back to us our lost,
our heights, our love. Oh magisterial light we will make without looks,
without sound bodies; oh red brocade unsighted, us all to transform, if
malformed we have been.
Dido remembers, and I stood at a window so dark-blue that trees cried
glory for all that existed, a color, and one light's riches, fulgent candle.
Nothing to be hidden from this feeling—is that what we seek? To found a
feeling which is already incipient. We have no colors to our forms, but we
cry out to each other in jeweled tones. These are not dictated woods,
renewed gifts or burning morrows: we have founded now. And we will push
it to deep enduring.

UNIDENTIFIED

When the image broke—

I keep seeing that as
        diamond shots—
even more
vocal inflections

You
nobody . . .

or anyone, hanging on
to the last-throb civilization,
gasping the last air

ghoul!

_____

There are no vendors
in my condition

                    Had
Sold you and sold you and sold you

maintaining artful
con upon nothing was.

_____

To You

You still think you're you, tough

able to get
your way. Because of money or
        dad
Weren't you appetizing?
A life as strenuous
        as strutting.
You could be a shit, alive
But in *this* kind of alive
everyone's a blood-lipped
mirrory wraith—recognize the world?
        not only this space

I'm not even
        making this up.

———————————

Don't know you, he
        says. I know
you, I say: you're a jerk
Come wait with us, we're
        waiting for
something: some sort of
        laminated lie.
Maybe it will work
maybe I'll just get back at
        you, by saying things.

———————————

All of us
conning
        each other till
the end.

There's got to be some-
        thing, you say

Does there?

_____

In this city of my voice could we
        become beautiful?

homo sapiens y va changer le monde
an ad for the ancient past

The men were eating each other.
        The king
was simply a cannibal; I
saw the dishes served to him, a
        man's face
cut off cooked, on a platter
pale, eyes closed. The serving man
replaced the lid and carried
the dish downstairs.

_____

I walk around holding
my coat close: sexless,
ghoulishly thin I was—
so I could disappear into

the world I "imagined":
where I could be
possessed by any
turn of voice I gave ear to.

Since the mondial war
had conquered the
dimension of mythology,
could I trash it there

damage it so hard
it would back down, a

chastened sea, and calm?

———————————————

Who do you know named
        Judgment? I ask
You have always
        hoped no one, but it is a
condition of these pages.
You are judged wanting of
        your trappings
Who the fuck are you now?

SAND

Repetition of sand: colored
      patterns till
nothing wins. I want to win
I don't exist; I have the skills
      to win.
Everything is still hidden.

    heart in sand.

———————

      Am
tearing you apart.
         This is no
    form of
protest: why protest against
    the long-gone
coward, your
      heart
        lowering the scale
      against Maat's feather?

———————

Voice: you are going to enter an
African country. Called Maat or Judgment.

I've been here for days, disposed to
cruel meditations. Dark forms pile up
in my heart to be weighed. Halfway through
the poem, I am another person.

Leave the drunk man at the table,

There is no consecutive order
Whatever you've done doesn't
        stop, or
start.

But haven't I already
        been here?
                You're
always here.

I have a ferret on a long leash pulling
me on. I have a ferret in a long lash
a lithe unpuling curious form: I have a
history if I choose it. Can I unchoose
recast it apply for another?

The ferret slips into a
        cage
it is a monkey's cage
then the monkey tears out its
        throat
my throat?
rip it out on my way to declaim
at the, who is your? history

Because Frat boys had to hang
Greek letters over
the Alamo. Is that my
        history? No. Almost
my throat.

—————————————

The Egyptians didn't understand
that Maat weighs your heart
        continuously.
That's why she's so tired. And
        why it hurts.

I have no throat for this aria

Do you recognize my heart?

You are the public, reading a
        book
wondering if it can be yours.
But I came here to be you,
long the leash pulled at my throat;
taking us to any last stand,
heart composed of tragic moments
        in sung patterns.
Who can stay near any more of his
        telling and drinking?
The man sinks in the rhymed world towards
the table poised
        to prop up our pose
but he's dreaming of Maat

—————————————

The dead woman's voice
    comes out of the CD
male version of
her fury: *her masterpiece*

How can Maat weigh *her*
    heart, it's
composed of his
    action, creation—
Once more, the ghoulish task
    of waiting
for righteous renewal: but
    all ghouls
are not women—

CAN'T I EVEN BE JUDGED?

LIGHT AROUND RIGHT SHOULDER

    ... all these things
look like they're from a
charnel house
            No
one of them
is my most precious gris-gris.

How do you know which one

It looks like knucklebones.

_____

Everyone is here but so in-
visibly. Their words cling to
me shaky pearl skins. It was
a lot of victims; exhaled
speech
       must become lucent

despite given to a
black
     metal wind.

_____

Forgiveness is recommended
by those who fear us—
For if all our energy
turned toward
the source of our
    misery,

Nothing you say would
        remain
nothing you've said into being;

the ghost of you unspared
        to the last
vapor.

Who had been tortured
centuries ago or now
someone standing over my shoulder
nods.

———————————

I had cut my wrist
        cooking
I had cut it in five
        places
Fucked up trying to
        cook
only to cook.

This cut is too deep so
        I'm crying
Do you know this feeling?

'Don't you have ordinary
        feelings?'

We are locating other
feelings—all the
unrecorded ones—and
building this city of them.

For we are each singular
cadavers; never were what
was said of us.

———————————

DO YOU HEAR ME?

All the assassins of
     my power
were mobilized that day—
they wanted the beauty
     of the blood that
she lay dead in, didn't they?

If not, why did they
     cause it
the war in her home town?

———————————

There is a lovely hissing
when you speak.

My aggravated pimp
would never have let me
     talk to you
in life, but now that
     I'm here, he
can't beat me. The rules
are different.

———————————

Do you have a sex when
        you're dead?
But I'm a ghoul, she said

She was eating in front of
        the poster
of her eating. She was
        gnawing the
meat from the knucklebones
        for my gris-gris

my most precious gris-gris.

WOMAN IN FRONT OF POSTER OF HERSELF

Said I shouldn't.
    Fingering me.
Everything I did.
A litter of chewed knucklebones

I've spread them out over the
rectangular floor as regularly as
I can; so I can account for them.

———————————

Her hands are crossed over
her breasts and each holds
a feather; her face has no features

Have I come to beg

What do I wish—to be
judged?

———————————

Is it an accumulation
of what I've said, that
counts, that I'm counting
is it all alphabet and abacus
everything rhymed?

———————————

You still don't have a face.

———————————

Suddenly *she* has the face of a
cat.
      No that's a different
goddess.

I tell you this
bloodthirsty
jaguar . . .

———————————

I haven't any idea what my word is, I
mean fault. Is it a word or an act. The
whole thrill is ripping me apart
                    Inside these
words there's nothing but a pumping
bloodsoaked . . .

but clearly, everything I said, did,
was a long shot

———————————

We didn't hear a word

What have you ever heard?

———————————

Now I'm here—black-caped in a
chair. Animal staring at me

I sink into your disaffected
ambiance to name.
What emotional
charges
have been laid on me from
earliest times
and my own
earliest
resulting in the bone strewn carpet

I had to grow the dice
of accounting to your love; for
you made me speak to you
lovingly; or did I do that naturally
oh just, bloodthirsty face
who doesn't have to understand.
I don't know who I'm speaking to
is pushing me

_____

Judgment maybe it's when being
fragile I
hallucinate you best

_____

I don't want to use my name!

"Where I was born we girls ran

free. and named ourselves,"
Justice says.

She may kill me,
it depends on whether she's hungry

MILLIONS OF US

Purportedly a chain of civilians, soldiers, voices
lice they were called. It is sometimes sufficient to beg
Lice creeping over one, kill them with a chemical;
then there are lice-ghosts everywhere. Glints of pearly
nails. The light of my beloved will keep me from noticing.
Trailer to keep her in; he asked me if I knew her 'auction name.'
Walked over the scorch; what are values when there's nothing here?
The wing of a dead soul grows into all the lace you see through,
foreigner, lice-ridden article of divestment. Splendid vices
pouring outcomes over the eager cash flow promotions.
So many of the dead came to me that their transparencies
covered my visage, I'm too near you. Don't you want to *see*?
We came from faraway camps, forsaking the human because it
broke our bodies into pieces for the torturer's pet, who
propositions you. There is always a slant on it. The trees *must*
go down; or light affects your eyes badly. We pleaded for an
adjustment, before we'd recognizably died. You
told me you were a heart, but you were guarding a tower. You
said you were a failure, but you helped destroy us.
Wings all over me, stuck to my skin, there's no point to it
why are you here when there's nothing? We just don't believe it.

Now not no never you. I wasn't you. You have to talk to me
my name is irretrievable. No one letting you go because you
are prized for not existing except as a body, now not.
No I don't exist, alighting and ghoulishly begging you for a
drop of your blood, a morsel of your flesh. Yes take some of
me, though there are so many others with flesh. But they're too
rich to give. I know they will never let you in, you beautiful
kids who haunt the corridors extending through
the invisible world, so you can find your way. So you can see
past the smoke of disastrous fear acting out of dreams:

it creeps everywhere. See how it took them over, for
they had no mind to stand against any fantasy the instigators
chose. Had no minds at all. When I was little, no one told
me I'd have to suffer. Who can be a child? And the ghoul
patiently explains how the wing of a word can extend till the
barrier is made, so they can't see us. If you say *beauty*, that
will be ignored, and we can hide. It was his name a long time ago,
before the auctions began. Her face then was large and younger.
She can be lice or ghoul. I want that, I don't want action. But I
will have to live off bits of you.

The new definition of witch is one who lets them eat you, if
they have to. Because you keep regenerating. Oh that's such an oldy,
and all that flying. Sometimes they do—the man who showed me a
few things sits all day. The teaching is to let them come as far as
inside you even, empty enough; I can hear them and render affection
Why, if there's nothing? Is this nothing? But you are destroyed
We shake all the time. You remind me of someone else I knew.
The wing is inscribed, *for involute*. Not to beg in the offering
of primal services, we have come here. No one would let us tell
anything but our bodily humiliations; had to do differently, not for
redemption, because we are more than redemption. I am my maker.
The shape formed by the bits of mirror glued on is unimportant.
They're inside my chest and stomach, and they glitter in there.
Then if light disattaches, comes up to be spoken, you
can see and you can hear. This is true because each of you has this
too. Has all the bright pieces inside: there was nothing else
left to be. Then I say it, like these pages, or how they would
love me for hosting them. The earliest people feared them,
and subsequent ones deny the dead. Why would I be afraid of
all the people dead and martyred? I thought you were talking
about words. You knew I wasn't.

Dido who had to be delivered from the wrong story:
I want you to know I'm no longer left over. What about our
library, nothing good left there? I want to read the fashion of when you
were old a long time ago. Gothic roses in the type; I'm an ancient
Had read every the book of before they arrested me.
I had crossed the black plain, I had held tears it was abrupt
to be walked in a herd pushing us, wherever we went to be shot, or
executed in the earlier style. It is a timeless death placed next to the
most beat-up books. Only a book can love me now. We're reading
without real eyes; I've read everything too, or in the tradition of
telling it is repeated within you what we did. We must have
been trying to make something as we are now, but why. You
have the ear for it. The light wants you to reply, asking if a
shore had been attained or if the language were Dutch or Swahili
I didn't know. It is how you raised the ground, like raising a child
every word that comes out of my mouth torn I'm responsible to
The wind foul pieces here tries to turn me from tenderness, the way
they killed us in the center of the city, that night. The bodies
floated in the river while I looked for other souls and saw my face
water damaged a new texture and how can I see? Potential
returning within its white petals and central whorl.

He couldn't believe someone would hate and betray. I
told him, but he refused to believe it; then I left the room.
This lace has to be made. Treason said the ghoul that
peculiar invention betrayal, how primal was that?
In Hesiod after the light, after chaos and lover. Said the armless
woman, said the one cut open, said the smallpoxed
the strewn children their bodies woven into the page
so I could find what they thought, even if babies only cry.
Those are the bodies when I was no longer alive but uplifted
butterfly of lace with an empty length to bifurcate my symmetry.
No I don't believe the lies of the live. I am a spot of light in
order to find out, hanging on because it wasn't revealed in
death. I know what happened to me, she said; bleeding I

lay there unblessed. Do I want a blessing now, or a god to
rebuild me? We have gone beyond god or new lives, or death, or
tribes. I am working on this lace light at present; I accept the
drop of sacrificial blood to propitiate me. One piece of you at a time
is all I need. I am letting you feed, I say, because I know this has
always been. You've been telling me for years
We needed you, if no one else did. We have this project to
change our silence into the beautiful city of a voice.

ALONG A SPECTRAL TRAIL

I am speaking to know the
        weight
of a passion
        Whose voice
Its

Can I identify

the worth of my
passions?

_____

I hurt you, you hurt me
wasn't nothing but a
        lace argument
who'd care?
wasn't like a whole field
        of bodies.

Whose passion did they
        satisfy dead?

Not even evolved past the
        fetal stage.
why fucking dress it up

_____

I can identify you by
        your blood.

Isn't that excellent
Or a little spit.
That's wonderful

You'll find out who I
        really am
throw me some raw meat
maybe you'll make love
        to me honey

it's the luck of the word
        though:
what's your name
who's your daddy

_____

I know what *I* do
I compel you to confront the
force of my words
to carry it wherever you walk

It's the only way I can have
something.

Do you need something

Or else a woman has nothing.

_____

Men have become addicted to
spying on fetuses, lodged in a tank,
through special glasses which give
them and the fetuses black bead eyes.

The men—scientists—keep trying not
to do it again, and then do. There
is a tag sentence, for the tank of fetuses,
taken from computer usage: "This is
only the range of experience."

———————————

Evolution

took
the passway to the
        side
signifying violence

Stuck in being
        smart enough
to have a calculator for
        the Holocaust.
Evolved into the computer.
"This is only the range of
        experience."

———————————

I found the deer's body; had I
        killed it?

I *had* to eat, the first time
        I killed it.
I stabbed the lovely animal
        myself. The deer

sang, 'When the mass of the
moment is opposite, love

lies back along a
spectral trail.'

———————————

We need for all of you to
be more beautiful.

We're asking for that
is that a lot

because I can't sew this
if you're just still ugly.

———————————

Pariah pattern lace I like.
He detested the canker I
        couldn't help
                conscripted particles
they herd us into
idea. It's an awful bad ar-
        rangement
You can sing of it. Your lips took
        place once
My lips took place
        once.
                Take place now

NO TO ANGEL

I started to dream awake
It was beautiful—as I
    began
to chant an old poem
on the edge
    of dream

Slip past the border. I have
    always been
this poet.
        Night
gold
    calling me to know
multiples of now.

———————————

To hurt the political

    Or would you

Come off the
chair sir. Ask the chairman
    to come off . . .

You have gone past your
    dead lover's marker.

He'll
    stay same

who's sane (same old
        joke—
ancient Baghdadian pa) . . .

Skimming over dreams.

_____

Walking the way
long way to go

        . . . a lot of things
I badly wanted not to be
        like.

_____

There was an angel I didn't
        care for . . .

have never
        trusted angels.

I found one of her white
cylindrical hairs
        dyed black

finally knew
she wasn't relevant.

_____

Songs and chants by the
beauty-making
        ghouls

to us is given a drop of
        your live beauty, to
feed us, who are the poetry.

I remember he caught a pigeon
and stuck it for a few drops of
blood. To sprinkle on the
ground, there in that dream.
        It was
in another lifetime.

—————————————

As beautiful as
            a raven, a fire, a
                fawn

the word 'treason' takes
        credit for achieving us.
We have betrayed all your
        religions
in order to
be alive, after our deaths, in
            this space

        it is lace counter to scheme.

The first thing, in the
beginning, was the lie.

—————————————

The motel for
        making sense
is where I
        go.

Everyone busy with dead
        hands/voices/senses

Dead sense swells.

Whatever you want that
        isn't a thing,
you can have.

No god. that's what I want.

——————————————

Cloister of pearlized shafts
        (arrow luster)
amid a lighter green.
        Figment
puts hand center of my chest
to say, 'there is a formal
        condition to
your body. Aren't figment.'

Clustering moments,
But you know when a
        moment
is

Seeing it through.

IN MOTEL/HANGAR/MOCK HOUSE

You,
trying to keep your pieces
                    in place.
You believe in your pieces
                    as
    pieces;
but you want to stay in
    control
theorizing about them
without falling to pieces.

It doesn't matter,
        asshole, doesn't
matter.

You can't lose you, you'll never

You are
an eye, an asshole.

———————————

The most violently founded
        of us
weeping to make shelter
        for
himself. in the center
of the convulsion
there.

        You asshole,
cut-glass eye.
If you touch yourself

right now you'll
bleed.

———————————

Yes it flattened out too much
Yes that's what we did to the world

———————————

What am I supposed to
        do, fall
in love with her father
        you
are always supposed to
        The seething

won't go away.

———————————

Hound your little adversaries.
Their special vicious masquerading
as humor or rapture, why not,

or maybe anesthetic other con job.
Like, says proudly, *this has no tone
        of voice.*
Then, I say,
I don't have to read it.

———————————

No you're supposed to
        fall in love with
her younger brother. Why?
        He has
connections
The rest of the men are pro-
        bably dead.

I'm dead too;

wants me to go away and
        leave you
hungry

not give any more drops of my
        blood
to you
but I will.

———————————

The WITCH is not a
        failure.
She is the name of
        holding it together

(more than you could ever
        do.)

———————————

In my origin song, I broke the king
and then I was sad; a giant he was too
tall, of stone; I shot shattering his head.

His mind never moved until I broke it
He had grown tall, or had been carved
in order to be perfect in our earliest
perception, until we too were rocky
and couldn't think. Why am I sad? I
have slain an art work; killed a statue
There are some forms you can't
fuck, you can only destroy. Faceless
he is a standup maimed memory
of a country where I was unhappy.

MOMENT

There was this moment
before. A long time before
I acted; before I did what I don't
discount

still there.

_____

I forgot I might ruin myself—and
before I did—

in the bloodspattered dress she
        sings best

before I did:

        someone's young dress.

_____

Windows blow open, the haunt
a torso

We wear
the same size nightgown

        any two women
might

Why must we
wear them
in this house

Windows blow open
to the haunt, but
I thought
that was me.

No she's
cut off at the torso

I am the one who
remembers her—*her*

I remember you.

———————————

We're in the wide vicious room. I
came in through the window I say.
Looking for ancient Judgment, and
only got an east coast house, full
of deadly forebears, oh those portraits,
like ourselves. We're supposed to
be the same woman.

———————————

Who needs a lower body now,

to reflect
brokenly
all
colors.

That was that night.
Arraigned on charges

It blows in
      as if I did it

it is the reflection of
the lay of it.

What I did or what
happened

wearing a young
dress, forget

got it at the factory?
      not from
you, here, where you
only believe
          this
passes.

What is the weight of
a passion
used? was it useful, or I
couldn't have gotten through

the window
of the mock house,
a mock body.

CITY OF VOICE

You had to turn the
          baby in to the authority.
     The dead woman watched.
Far
         because not seen
     the fate is too far from some
How can I show you
         how I happened
   and remain?
I don't know why the guns
         had to tell us
     everything; as if it were *only*
a city. A power position. If
         no one you care about
     judges you, you can kill anyone.
I have a drop of your blood in my mouth
         so I can
     continue to speak. If you are
dead, a soldier child, of violence
         what is the
     name of your life? Answer me.
I am not found. Let me find
         you. I am not to be
     appeased. I killed in the
weight of the real air, I was small
         I sank from sight; it
     was logical. The earth
hadn't grown me high enough
         a fate. There is still
     a gloss on these gloves.
I need to hear you better. You
         can't love me. There
     is a thread of being from the first

that I am. I will be that. No
            intercession offered.
        I wanted a better gun; now
I can't want that, what can I
            want
        the assassin I?
You won't have to remember
            we're making a ring of
        uncontested lace, to fill memory's place.
The origin ornamented with gold
            discourse of
        what is birdlike arising
from the east. An
            owed part? No.
        My name was pierced I cannot
owe. She took a grenade down to hell
            a ball of wild-fire
        for all who would die in his hall.
Yes, I did that. I killed many
            they are martyrs to
        the gratitude of Force. A kind
of power. Lady has none, though to
            her milk and blood
        it be attributed; mine would never
cure—have cured—you. Only words
            can cure us now
        our power to remain, which
has as its source its own being
            pure self
        My granite foundlings. Killers the lace
loves.

You think you should know who
            is speaking: if we

name ourselves we're owned.
Now that you can't see a mark
        on my body, will you
    listen to me?
Front and back covers, matching
        You can hear
    me without knowing who I am.
Heal the dead? I am known
        as the quarrel or the souvenir
    How can you heal such abstraction?
A woman entered
        Everyone was saying
    'mankind' a frigid
insult; it's lasted since I've been
        dead into the rot, freight
    of the ship
of a death whose star is not to be in
        my lace. Gendered death
    Your old frieze
dirt refuses; we will not grow
        from our past.
    Will the dead child grow?
You had been counseled to
        kill him. After all, he
    had a gun; begin with death not
the throwing away of weapons. This
        head still frenzied
    not calm in intricacy, but
mad of it: I can't bear the pattern
        that's happened: let me go
    into my own death. You don't
have your own. No one *deserves*,
        and we're not bound in
    godly jurisdiction.
No one knows what's fitting but
        if she did,
    how could she endure it? Can we

change from being crushed to
            pattern light? Unlatcheted ...
      nothing wrong with pretty words.
I believed your book never you.
            I must turn in
      the baby so they can judge her female
· And I take her and run from that
            land, you have already
      found her wanting; I am running
until I die. Am I still running? No, she is
            sweet a book
      of art, all magic
My will still alive in free space
            could seek a
      grave. Truth formed in un-
varying color, blood of
            influence flowing
      You were faithful and frank—
I was destitute often; too
            soon they died. You'll
      forget. All the talk has been
of remembrance. See my love a
            light, I don't want to
      I don't want a light of yours.

I loved you and so why not anyone
            I don't want to call to you
      It isn't your business any-
more. But we're here now. This air can
            still hurt, with flat
      crystal foliage we're making.
If living had to be about the body
            who made it so? In our old
      language we'd say we're free, but the words

are empty when you're free. He got
                more money—you got more
        money than I did—
for your sex art. I forgot to bring mine
                to the abbatoir: it wouldn't
        have helped. They slaughtered us
even though we loved each other. No god.
                No. No religion. You don't
        have to wonder if you
should be doing something else. Was there
                one I loved, doesn't make sense
        Is the pattern too cold
I'm burning in it; that other fire
                someone made me do it
        No I don't believe you. The sun
is all I am. He got money for his
                pornography; I wanted to
        sell eros too, because I would have
love then, if that was money.
                All I had to exchange; which one
        They blend. What was powerful
was any vision: sold myself for eyes
                Have too many now
        No *so* many, so you don't need to
watch it, here in the lace, putting
                your hands you may not have
        to show the redemptive power
of sex any more. Remember
        all the
        feelings inside that no one said
or would have let you have.
                I could bear the ones
        I didn't understand; the others
were subject to approval. I am combing
                them, parting them
        from faith. You
could have infatuated a planet, you'd

say. You could have
infuriated a lamprey. You You
From my body's unconfused
silk I drew my mind
up a ladder from flatland to
an open opera. I didn't I was
dismembered. Who
loved me? You lurked and struck
No god. There's all us ornately
an eagle, as chosen
now in our art. Your pieces the
precious stones giving power to
our sensible
fabric. Touch
this sex so bitten by the weather, touch
a thorn, an
umber navel. Be true.

Each a sea, in all the seas:
a city. I'm fighting
with you, before. The Three
Fates crochet with brown yarn
they have brown hair
pulled back in a style of some
century—do we have centuries? Every
time I loved you it was
now in all the seas
The theme of my stay is the
fertilization of the
self. O raped one, they dragged
her down. He took her to his world
but I've founded
the city, unangelic eyes, it's snowing
in front of them, and on the white ocean.

I've found
you. You can't have me. Was I
fated? You don't know
how to moor.
This city isn't static. I shouldn't
have been given three glasses.
Don't find me. But
this is forever
He tried to keep us in only one part
of the manor.
Grim one, who betrayed you?
It was a collective order, out of the
unthinking
bounded lake, where we'd rot
Refusing to believe the future, the
dark of his men
a cannibal god.
Each a sea, in all the seas. To
fertilize the self you
you . . .
Calling to a city. Don't remember now.
I'm losing sight of
the stark tower, in the snow, that I'd
never seen. Leave
the champagne. I rested it
against the house of
the Fates, so tender, young ones intent
on this work
it was all about love, now they pretend
that it wasn't. The power to kill
belonged to someone—
but I had no power, except for
this onrushing now. Keeps saying
go back oh I
won't climb down. There are
no levels here.
You lost your

purse, you lost your conception of
yourself. I've fertilized another self
        You don't ever have
        to testify again. I
don't have to be for or against you
        What if you hurt me?
        It isn't possible now,
because there are no gods. Only a
        city, of so many fates
        gone, unremembering presences.

THE HUMAN GHOUL

This lady in me is
        Justice,
an abstraction live

'Oh I love you
        when there's
blood in your hair and you
come at me railing.'

I once entered everywhere
as dispassion, now have
        become
bloody from judging
the foul acts of human hands.

I've got bloody hair so
you can love me.

I've got a tone of voice.

_____

He hid the body in another
        body;
the second corpse, shrinking,
disappeared into the first one
Or did the first disappear into the
        second?

A very tall man, he
said he was a writer
        but

not a good
        writer.

You're not a good
        writer, I said,
because
        you aren't
good.

I am speaking to you, with your
violent wish to be loved.

———————————

Someone
has to understand
what has happened

before she disappears—

it doesn't matter
what she disappears
into—heaven, nirvana

someone has
to understand what's
been going on

from
        here.

———————————

What is a feeling. Is it what
happens. He leaves her.

Someone has to say what
happened. When did it start?

he asked. *You made me wear blood
but I thought I must want to.* He
left and I wanted to find him;
he left because I was talented.

———————————

A feeling is what is said to
          happen.
Change a feeling by
          telling
what happens. It's what you
          say.

A self has a stain on its
          floor or
a long dark cloth
Dido, anyone, walks into the
self, rejuvenates the
          founding

in a world that celebrates
          war

where all are ghouls.

I'm the one who sees it

You have a lot of change, the
          man
said, having counted it, It's
          almost too much.

I put it in my
            purse
and crossed the avenue.

————————————

I had bloody hair so you
would love me, too old
            now
to be loved or to wash out
            the blood.
I am all of the faces of
            Justice
broken as I exit the
mirror falling in pieces
            behind
me again and again. The

figment told me
I was now changed a
            total stranger
looking out of this body.

CITY OF GHOSTLY FESTIVALS

Try to find
the center of night. this city

A hear break, I can't *hear* it.

Dido the appropriated victim
sets all the bottles rattling
in the wind of our agains.

I wanted a different again.

It's different.

———————————

The syllabary
     of my
sins
a
thing Maat
flicks
     into
the river
running
judgment

a million literal years of.
I'm sick of judging your carnage,
    she says,

you are all left alone
    with it.

———————————

Dido's job
for two thousand years
has been to
        commit suicide

after
her death, and after
the Romans destroy her
        foundation.

———————————

The witch's job. is to change
        time
which runs in short lines
        between
events like innumerable
        falls of cities

is watching me. But it isn't.

If you change the nature of
        events
do you change time?

Event: I sat down to
talk to everyone
        who had ever lived.

———————————

'My country
is broken and it can't be fixed'

time loved so
femina-hating Rome
        always falling

I, the witch, pardon no one

instead, I change Dido's job.

———————————

Man with whom everything is
        boring
everything he does and that one
        does with him
is boring. One is condemned
to be part of his
        boring world.

There is another man
with whom one's condemned
        to be
duplicitous
Everything's a cheat a scam
in the big-guy road-house world
Help him tell lies. wear special
        clothes
for that.

———————————

THIS WAS HOW I BROKE IT

They told me I couldn't have
     it—time—so
I took it.
I put him
     away
who had withered to a doll.

―――――――――

We ghouls waiting outside of time . . .

Dido to poem: Do all my remembering
     now
so city continues.
Do we accept it says voice
He became too old to be wise; we
had to step outside him
and into knowledge
of poetry, the ghoulish, timeless state.

―――――――――

This poem, the poem,
always
my real country

About the Author

Alice Notley is the author of over thirty collections of poems, including the now classic epic *The Descent of Alette* (1996), *Mysteries of Small Houses* (1998), *Grave of Light: New and Selected Poems 1970–2005* (Wesleyan, 2006), *Reason and Other Women* (2010), and *Culture of One* (2011). She is the recipient of the Griffin Poetry Prize, the *Los Angeles Times* Book Award for Poetry, the Shelley Memorial Award from the Poetry Society of America, an Academy Award from the American Academy of Arts and Letters, and the Academy of American Poets' Lenore Marshall Prize. For many years she has lived and written in Paris, France.